Opening the Door

A Treatment Model for Therapy with Male Survivors of Sexual Abuse

Opening the Door

A Treatment Model for Therapy with Male Survivors of Sexual Abuse

Adrienne Crowder, M.S.W.

Clinical Consultant: Rob Hawkings, M.A., M.E.S., M.B.A.

BRUNNER/MAZEL *Publishers* • NEW YORK

Library of Congress Cataloging-in-Publication Data

Crowder, Adrienne.
    Opening the door : a treatment model for therapy with male survi-
vors of sexual abuse / Adrienne Crowder ; clinical consultant, Rob
Hawkings.
        p.   cm.
    Includes bibliographical references.
    ISBN 0-87630-754-3
    1. Adult child sexual abuse victims—Mental health. 2. Adult child
sexual abuse victims—Counseling of. 3. Adult child sexual abuse
victims—Rehabilitation. 4. Male sexual abuse victims—Mental
health. 5. Male sexual abuse victims—Counseling of. 6. Male sexual
abuse victims—Rehabilitation. 7. Child sexual abuse—Treatment.
I. Hawkings, Rob.
    RC569.5.A28C76   1995
    616.85'836906—dc20   94-43270
                                                                             CIP

Published by
BRUNNER/MAZEL, INC.
19 Union Square West
New York, New York 10003

Manufactured in the United States of America
10 9 8 7 6 5 4 3 2 1

This book is dedicated to Christopher Crowder

Contents

Acknowledgments

Researching and writing this book would have been impossible without the help and support of a great many people.

Generous financial support was provided by the Family Violence Prevention Division of Health and Welfare Canada (under FVDS#4887-06-91-088). Carole Miron and Giselle LaCroix administered this project on behalf of Health and Welfare Canada with efficiency, patience, and courtesy.*

The management of Family and Children's Services of Waterloo Region granted me a three-month leave of absence to work on this book. Jim Phillips and Del Armbruster carefully ensured that the project stayed within its budget.

Susan Waterman and Fran Kolentsis took on the responsibility for locating written resources on male survivors of sexual abuse and they performed the task admirably. Rob Hawkings brought his clinical expertise and editorial scrutiny to this project. James Morgan made recommendations that became integral to the organization of the text. His willingness to listen to my excitement and frustration over the year and a half that I worked on this book, his ideas and suggestions, and his emotional support were all of inestimable value. Susan Lawrence edited the final draft of the text and her suggestions enhanced its overall quality. Joan Laing lent her desktop publishing skills to the project to make the final text accessible and readable. To all these people I give my heartfelt thanks.

Lastly, I would like to acknowledge the contribution of the 41 therapists who generously shared their knowledge about therapy with male survivors with me. It was always a pleasure to talk with these clinicians about their work and I was often touched by their compassion and skill. I believe that my most sincere thanks is expressed by passing on their ideas to others and sharing their collective wisdom.

---

*Findings and opinions expressed are those of the authors and not necessarily those of the department.

Chapter 1

Introduction

Sexual abuse is an activity that is perpetrated in secret. The offender is often in a position of trust, and always in a position of power, in relation to his or her victim. The victim acquiesces to the authority of the offender because he or she is threatened or seduced into compliance. Often a victim's cognitive and affective immaturity renders him or her unable to appropriately judge the potential risk of the behaviors that constitute the abuse.

In many ways the therapeutic process is isomorphic to that of abuse. Therapy occurs under a mantle of confidentiality. Clients enter therapy in good faith, with the expectation that a therapist will have their best interests at heart. Therapists are invested with the authority to determine the kinds of interventions they believe will best assist their clients' recovery. As in situations of abuse, clients generally have no immediate way to judge the long-term effects of their therapy or the skills of their therapist.

The difference between therapy and abuse, however, lies in the fact that ideally therapy is driven by the clients' needs, whereas abuse ignores the victims' needs. If therapy is to be effective in restoring clients' autonomy and well-being, therapists must manage treatment in ways that do not suggest or replicate the dynamics of the original abuse.

Opening the Door has been written to assist clinicians who work with, or are intending to work with, male survivors of sexual abuse. Throughout the text, the parallel processes of therapy and abuse are discussed; the important distinctions between these two processes that ensure that therapy is a healing rather than a harmful experience form the basis of the treatment model that is presented here.

The raw material that forms the basis of this book was gathered from interviews with 41 therapists who have developed expertise in working with male survivors of sexual abuse. The text discusses both the similari-

1

ties and differences in approach that these therapists bring to their work. It also presents applied interventions that they have developed to enhance their work.

This book is written for mental health practitioners (therapists, social workers, psychiatric nurses, doctors, crisis center workers, etc.) who are offering therapeutic services to adolescent and/or adult male survivors of sexual abuse. The information presented here is not meant to be prescriptive. Rather, it is meant to stimulate your own thinking and creativity. You are invited to take this information and improve on it by adapting it to suit your own therapeutic style and experience.

Throughout the text, I assume that each person's recovery process from childhood sexual trauma is unique. In addition, I assume that the kinds of formal treatment that are discussed here form only one part of any individual's healing journey. Although this text, of necessity, deals with the political and cultural components of abuse, its primary focus is on the personal and psychological aspects of recovery from sexual trauma.

DEFINITION OF SEXUAL ABUSE

Throughout this book, the term "sexual abuse" will be used to describe overt or covert sexual behavior between two individuals when the following conditions exist:

1. the nature of the sexual act(s) is developmentally inappropriate for at least one of the participants;
2. the balance of power and authority (meaning psychological power, economic power, role status power, etc.) between the two individuals is unequal; and
3. the two individuals have an established emotional connection (such as that between a child and a caregiver, or a child and authority figure).

Any definition of sexual abuse necessarily carries culturally determined values and beliefs about sexuality, self-determination, and social roles. In the broadest sense, sexual abuse can be defined as:

...sexual activities that a child does not understand, to which a child cannot give informed consent or which violate the social taboos of society. (Krugman, 1986, as cited in Banning, 1989, p. 566)

The nature of the sexual acts that constitute sexual abuse vary along a continuum of intrusiveness. Activities such as voyeurism, viewing pornographic materials, or age-inappropriate behavior regarding physical health (for instance, checking to see if a 12-year-old's penis is "growing properly") fall on one end of the continuum. Sadistic and ritualistic abuse constitute the other end.

It must be noted that a client's perception of the intrusiveness of any specific sexual activity is subjective. His perceptions may change as he redefines his childhood experience through his adult understanding. It is the client's experience that needs to be addressed in therapy rather than whether or not the behavior is objectively considered intrusive.

LANGUAGE

This text focuses on therapeutic work with male survivors of childhood sexual trauma. For the sake of accuracy and simplicity, I use the pronoun "he" when referring to victims or clients.

The terms "victim" and "survivor" are both commonly used in abuse-related discussions and literature. Historically, these terms were adopted by the feminist movement to describe victims of rape. Rape victims are violently attacked during an incident that is outside the normal events of their lives. With sexual abuse, however, the trauma is usually repetitive and often seductive. Generally, the abuse is integrated into the child's life and, in one way or another, his beliefs, feelings, behavior, and sexuality are conditioned by the abuse. Hence, to describe someone as a "victim" or a "survivor" of sexual abuse can minimize the internalized dysfunction that can occur as a result of the long-term and pervasive nature of the abuse. These terms also run the risk of overgeneralizing a client's identity as a survivor of childhood sexual trauma, thereby discounting those aspects of the person that currently function in healthful and productive ways.

Given the limitations of language and a need to be succinct, I will use the terms "victim" and "survivor" throughout this text. However, the limitations of these terms noted above cannot be overlooked. Ultimately, both "victim" and "survivor" perpetuate an association with a history of abuse (Hunter, 1990). It is to be hoped that after successful therapy a client will identify the impact of his abuse as only a part of his life's journey and not as its totality; ideally, he will see himself as "someone who was abused as a child" rather than as a "victim" or "survivor" of abuse. "The ultimate goal of therapy ought to be to transcend survivorship.... The individuality of personhood must be paramount" (Hunter & Gerber, 1990, p. 83). Readers are asked to bear in mind that the terms "victim" or "survivor" are used in this volume as a convenient shorthand rather than as empirical descriptors.

Throughout the text, the 41 clinicians who were interviewed about their work with male survivors are referred to as "the contributors" or "the clinicians participating in this research."

RESEARCH METHOD

The material presented in this text has been compiled from two primary sources: namely, interviews with clinicians who provide therapy to sexually abused males and the current literature (most notably books and journal articles). The contributors who participated in this research were a nonprobability, purposive sample of clinicians who have therapeutic experience with male survivors of sexual abuse.

Data collection occurred in the following sequence: first, computer and library searches located relevant written materials about sexually abused males. Second, North American authors of books or journal articles were sent a letter outlining the nature of this research and inviting them to participate in it. In addition, these writers were asked to provide the names of other clinicians whom they knew to be working with male survivors, and these clinicians were subsequently contacted. Third, all the clinicians who agreed to participate in this research were sent a questionnaire to gather information on their clinical orientation, the demographics of their client population, and the resources they use when working with male survivors. (For a copy of this questionnaire, please see Appendix A.) Fourth, the written questionnaire was followed by a semistructured telephone interview to gather more in-depth information about each contributor's clinical practice and specific interventions and techniques used. These phone interviews were conducted during the autumn of 1992 and the winter of 1993.

In total, 58 clinicians throughout Canada and the United States were approached and asked to take part in this research. Of these, 41 agreed to participate. Their names are listed in Appendix B. Thirty-one contributors returned the written questionnaire.

Thirty-two of the contributors are male; nine are female. The majority of the contributors have professional training in psychology, social work, or marriage and family therapy; however, clinicians with backgrounds in nursing and massage therapy are also represented. The contributors work in a variety of mental health settings, including community mental health clinics, family therapy agencies, hospitals, rape crisis centers, sex offender treatment programs, and private practice.

Contributors were asked to identify both their years of experience in providing sexual abuse treatment in general and sexual abuse treatment to male survivors in particular. As anticipated, given the greater cultural awareness of female victimization, the contributors had more years of clinical experience working with sexual abuse in general (providing therapy to female victims and their families) than with male victims in particular. To summarize:

- 68% of the contributors had provided general sexual abuse treatment for more than eight years;
- 23% had provided general sexual abuse treatment for between six and eight years; and
- 9% had provided general sexual abuse treatment for fewer than five years.

With regard to male survivors:

- 32% of the contributors had provided sexual abuse treatment to this population for more than eight years;
- 42% had provided sexual abuse treatment to male survivors for between six and eight years; and
- 26% had provided sexual abuse treatment to male survivors for fewer than five years.

Although some contributors specialize in working with a specific developmental group, many work with a variety of ages:

- 93% of contributors offer therapy to adult male survivors (clients over 25 years of age);
- 90% work with young adults (aged 20–25 years);
- 58% work with adolescent male survivors (13–19 years of age);

- 35% work with latency-aged children (6–12 years of age); and
- 16% work with preschool boys under the age of five.

Contributors were asked to identify the different therapeutic modalities they offer to male survivors of sexual abuse:

- 97% of the contributors offer individual therapy;
- 77% offer group therapy; and
- 52% offer couple and/or family therapy.

Some contributors also offer regular workshops for male survivors and/or they provide regular training to other professionals regarding the treatment of male survivors of sexual abuse.

LIMITATIONS OF THIS RESEARCH

Gathering the primary data for this book was a journalistic process rather than a scientific one. My intention in compiling this material was to create a practical resource for clinicians who work with male survivors of sexual abuse. Qualitative and exploratory research methods were used to meet this goal.

The contributors were located by virtue of either having published material on the subject of male sexual abuse survivors or knowing someone who had published in this area. Clearly some very knowledgeable practitioners may have been overlooked because they have not written about their work with male survivors or because they did not come to my attention during the initial stages of the research. In addition, some seasoned clinicians who were asked to participate in this research were prevented from doing so because of other work demands.

Therapy is a dynamic human interaction. It is by nature fluid and experiential. Translating therapeutic concepts and experience into written form necessarily entails some loss. Nevertheless, it is my hope that the treatment model described in this book will assist therapists in their work with male survivors.

ORGANIZATION OF THE TEXT

The remainder of this text is organized into 11 chapters (with seven appendices). Chapter 2 is called "Prevalence, Impacts, and Issues" and presents information about the frequency of male sexual victimization, the effects of this victimization on the individual, and the issues that victims typically bring into therapy.

Chapter 3 presents a four-phase treatment model for male survivors. These phases are called Breaking Silence, the Victim Phase, the Survivor Phase, and the Thriver Phase. The typical therapeutic tasks of each of these stages of therapy are outlined and discussed.

Chapter 4 outlines essential processes that pertain to all therapeutic modalities (individual, group, etc.) when one is treating male survivors of sexual abuse. Contracting with clients, assessment guidelines, and evaluation methods are discussed.

Chapters 5, 6, and 7 focus on individual therapy with male survivors, examining the Victim, Survivor, and Thriver phases of therapy, respectively. Interventions that the contributors have developed for use during each of these treatment phases are intertwined with general theoretical considerations.

Chapter 8 outlines a two-stage group treatment model for male survivors. Therapeutic issues such as contraindicators for group treatment and interventions that can be used in male survivor groups are presented.

Chapter 9 looks at several critical issues that are relevant to the treatment of male survivors. Engagement strategies, therapeutic impasses, and client/therapist gender dynamics are identified and explicated.

Chapter 10 focuses on the therapeutic process as it applies to adolescent male survivors. The ways in which the treatment process needs to be tailored to the developmental needs of this group are noted and discussed.

Because therapy is an interactive process and the therapist is as much a player in the therapeutic journey as the client, Chapter 11 discusses issues that pertain to the therapist rather than to the client.

Lastly, Chapter 12 presents resources (written and video resources, as well as training resources) that both therapists and clients can use to enhance the process of healing from sexual trauma.

Chapter 2

Prevalence, Impacts, and Issues

This chapter presents information about the prevalence of male sexual victimization, and discusses many of the reasons why attempts to establish an accurate picture of this phenomenon are problematic. Ways in which the experience of being sexually traumatized can impact on male victims are discussed, and the primary variables that generally act as predictors regarding the severity of the resultant pathology are identified. Finally, the primary differences between male and female sexual victimization are examined using both empirical research and clinical experience to inform the discussion.

ESTIMATES OF PREVALENCE

Cultural and social myths shape our ability to acknowledge many of the abusive and exploitative realities that exist in our culture. Sexual abuse, especially the sexual abuse of male children, has been invisible in our society until very recently.

In Freud's time father-daughter incest could not be accepted. Child physical abuse was only recognized and acknowledged in the 1960s and child sexual abuse in the mid 1970s. Not until the 1980s were male victims recognized and studied and their victimization found to be more frequent than previously recognized. (Banning, 1989, p. 569)

It is difficult to accurately estimate the prevalence of male sexual victimization for a variety of reasons. Researchers who "...attempt to determine the number of abuse cases within the general population (prevalence), report rates varying between 3% and 31% for males...."(Finklehor et al., 1986, as cited in Dimock, 1988, p. 203). An increase in the reported incidence rate of sexually abused males is also noted: "While the reports of both male and female victims have risen, the proportion of males rose from 15.7% of the total in 1980, to 21.7% in 1984 (American Humane Association, 1986)" (Dimock, 1988, p. 203). In Canada, in 1984, the Badgley Report found that 33% of men are sexually victimized at some point in their lives, that 75% of these assaults occur to boys under the age of 17, and that 25% of these assaults can be considered serious offenses chargeable under the Canadian Criminal Code (Bruckner & Johnson, 1987, p. 81).

Estimates of prevalence vary from study to study. A 1989 study of 592 American male college students from two different geographic regions determined that 15% of the students from the midwestern campus and 13% of the students from the southeastern campus "described at least one sexually abusive experience in childhood" (Fromuth & Burkhart, 1989, p. 536). A representative national sample of 2,972 American male college students found that:

Seven point three percent of the men reported a childhood experience that met at least one of the following three criteria for sexual abuse: (1) existence of age discrepancy between the child and perpetrator, (2) use of some form of coercion to obtain participation by the victim, and/or (3) a perpetrator who was a care giver or authority figure. (Risin & Koss, 1987, p. 309)

Clearly, although empirical studies have generated quantitative data identifying the problem of male sexual abuse, prevalence figures can only be estimated. The general problem of determining the extent of male sexual abuse can be summarized as follows:

Many or even most sex crimes are not reported. Therefore, determining the actual number of crimes is impossible, regardless of whether the victim is male or female. (Freeman-Longo, 1986, p. 411)

FACTORS AFFECTING THE REPORTING OF MALE SEXUAL ABUSE

The many factors complicating the reporting process for male victims of sexual abuse will be discussed in three categories:

(1) research-related factors;
(2) the impact of cultural beliefs and stereotypes; and
(3) clinically-related factors.

Research-Related Factors

Studies that attempt to determine the prevalence of male sexual abuse arrive at different estimations partly because they operationalize the definition of sexual abuse in study-specific ways. There is no standard definition of sexual abuse that comprehensively addresses sex, age, cultural, and regional differences (Risin & Koss, 1987; Urquiza & Keating, 1990). Hence, each study has a unique definition of sexual abuse and, in effect, measures different kinds of experience.

The samples that different studies draw upon are not standardized. Some research uses nonclinical populations such as college students, while other studies draw from clinical populations such as adolescents who are currently in treatment or adults who are imprisoned for sex-related crimes. Clearly, data describing these different populations will reflect experiences that are biased by unique variables. In addition, methodologies for data collection (i.e., self-reported questionnaires, face-to-face interviews, telephone surveys, etc.) vary from study to study, thus affecting the degree of reliability of the data. Hence "...differences in reported prevalence rates are more a reflection of the method of data collection than of the number of children who were sexually abused" (Urquiza & Keating, 1990, p. 96).

The Impact of Cultural Beliefs and Stereotypes

The underreporting of the sexual abuse of male children is often a reflection of cultural beliefs about gender roles and socialization. Certain actions, such as male sexual victimization, remain hidden because cultural myths and values shape the ways in which they are understood.

Myth of Male Self-Reliance

In his discussion of this issue, Finklehor (1984) says "the male ethic of self-reliance...has tended to portray youthful male sexuality in very positive, adventuresome terms...[and is] partly responsible for the serious underreporting of sexual victimization experiences involving boys" (p. 152).

The belief that males are always powerful and able to fend for themselves has created a mythology that implies that if a boy or man admits to being victimized he is seen as less than male. Our culture has no mythology to identify the process of male victimization and boy victims are emasculated by this bias. They are either seen as being like a woman and therefore feminized, as being powerless and therefore flawed, or as being interested in sex with men and therefore homosexual. None of these interpretations of victimization is a useful option for a boy who has been sexually abused and is trying to make sense of this experience.

Whether male children are abused by male or female perpetrators or both, the cultural interpretation of the event often minimizes its impact or puts responsibility for the abuse onto the victim (Sepler, 1991).

Myth of Sexual Initiation

Boys who are abused by a male are often seen as having engaged in homosexual acts for pleasure; this interpretation can be held by the victim himself, especially if, during the abuse, his penis responded to the sexual stimulation by becoming erect (Dimock, 1988; Struve, 1990; Urquiza & Keating, 1990).

It is worth noting that several journal articles (Sandfort, 1984; Tindall, 1978) discuss the exploitive nature of sexual relations between adults and children and argue that "...with the right circumstances (privacy, degree of sexual arousal, etc.), the first sexual relationship [between a male adult and a male child] occurred as a result of mutual desires" (Tindall, 1978, p. 380). This analysis of sexual acts between male adults and male children as consensual sexual experiences, without regard to the power and control issues that are involved, emphasizes the cultural blinders that permit continued sexual exploitation of children. Statements such as the following actively ignore the developmental differences in sexual needs and sexual expression that exist between adults and children.

Future research into pedophilia should not a priori categorize the adults in pedosexual contacts as offenders and the children as victims, labelling all pedosexual contact as abuse or misuse. Pedophiliac relationships may best be viewed by the researcher initially as simply another variety of human relationship. (Sandfort, 1984, p. 140)

Such statements clearly point out the difficulty that some male victims of sexual abuse face when they begin to identify and examine their experience of sexual abuse and are met with attempts to redefine this abuse as consensual sexual activity.

Our culture promotes the belief that all sexual activity is good for men, no matter what its context. Images from advertising, television, and cinema often portray sexual activities in which the "emotional reactions of male victims...are seriously distorted when compared to those of real-life victims" (Trivelpiece, 1990, p. 67). When sexual abuse is heterosexual and a sexually mature female victimizes a boy, he may have difficulty recognizing this as abuse, since the cultural interpretation of this event is that he "got lucky." In movies such as "The Summer of '42," sexual abuse is romanticized and represented as sexual initiation (Trivelpiece, 1990).

Myth of Female Innocence

Boys who are abused by women or girls also face social myths that can prevent their abuse from being identified. Cultural gender biases perpetuate the belief that women in general, and mothers in particular, are nurturing. Mothers have cultural permission to touch their children. When this touch is sexualized, sometimes under the guise of medical or caretaking rituals, a boy may have difficulty recognizing these behaviors as abusive. Because he is also subject to the cultural myth that women's touch is nurturing rather than sexual, he may be unable to discern that the sexual behaviors gratified his female abuser's needs rather than his own.

Cultural biases skew the ways in which activities are seen and the same activities are viewed differently depending upon whether they are performed by a man or a woman. This double standard often results in blindness to inappropriate sexual interaction between an adult women and a child.

There is a widespread societal belief that women cannot be sexually abusive to their children and at worst their behavior is labelled as seductive and not harmful. The same behaviour in a father is labelled child molestation. (Banning, 1989, p. 567)

Myth of Contact Contamination

The popular belief is that male victims of sexual abuse automatically become sexual offenders. While it is true that some sexual offenders were themselves victims of sexual abuse, the commission of sexual offenses is caused by complex variables which cannot be narrowed down to the single variable of previous sexual victimization (Freund, Watson, & Dickey, 1990). However, the cultural stereotype that victims of sexual abuse become offenders stops some victims from disclosing their abuse histories.

Clinically-Related Factors

Several aspects of the social service system act against the disclosure of male sexual victimization. Foremost amongst these is the fact that child protection agencies tend to deal with cases of intrafamilial sexual abuse, where they are mandated to ensure children's safety within their family systems. In his student survey, Finklehor (1984) found that, "Boys are more likely than girls to be victimized by someone outside the family" (p. 166). In fact, approximately 83% of the persons who victimized the male students in this survey were nonfamily members (Finklehor, 1984). Thus, acts of sexual abuse perpetrated against male victims, if they are reported at all, tend to be reported to the police or the criminal justice system, not to child protection or treatment agencies. This lack of societal recognition of male victims' needs for treatment and protection perpetuates victims' silence. Male victims are unlikely to disclose their sexual abuse when they have little to gain from making their experience public.

As will be discussed later in this chapter, victims of childhood sexual trauma often repress or forget their abuse-related memories. This primitive defense structure reduces the likelihood of disclosure of abuse by a victim. Even when explicit memories are present, if a therapist or child protection worker is uncomfortable asking questions about the abuse or presents questions in such a way that the child does not connect the question to his abuse, the abuse may not be reported (Hunter, 1990a).

Awareness of the issue of male sexual victimization in the professional therapeutic community is limited by the same factors that affect the culture as a whole. Until recently, professional literature and journal articles have focused on the prevalence of male sexual victimization rather than on the impact of sexual abuse on male victims or on models and methodologies of healing male survivors. An absence of information about how to work with male survivors has left many clinicians uncomfortable with or unaware of the male survivors in their caseloads. A lack of questioning about the possible occurrence of abuse can result in an absence of disclosure on a client's part.

In summary, there are many reasons why the full extent of male sexual abuse is relatively unknown and probably underreported.

> ...with males being even more reluctant than females to admit their own victimization, it is left to our imagination to conclude just what the full extent of male victimization is. Certainly it is greater than reports now indicate. (Blanchard, 1987, p. 20)

IMPACTS AND ISSUES FOR MALES WHO HAVE BEEN SEXUALLY ABUSED

Survivors of sexual abuse generally experience multiple and complex repercussions from this trauma. All parts of the self—physical, mental, emotional, and spiritual—arc affected by the abuse and all of these parts can express abuse-related symptoms and effects.

Abuse-related symptoms are experienced in both the short and long term. Some symptoms (such as physical bruises and cuts, some sexually transmitted diseases, emotional shock, or misdirected aggression) are crisis based and their impact is short term. Other symptoms (such as distorted cognitions or low self-esteem) are more deeply internalized by the victim and have a much longer-term impact (Evans, 1990).

Often, sexual abuse is accompanied by other forms of abuse and neglect, so that the trauma from the sexual abuse cannot be viewed in isolation. It is not always possible to determine the origin of symptoms that have multiple roots; however, as Olsen (1990) notes:

> From either an anecdotal self-report method or using valid, reliable instrumentation and comparative methodology, it was found that men who sought psychotherapy and had been sexually abused as children inside or outside their homes were far more psychologically disturbed than were other male therapy clients.... (p. 148)

There are some researchers who argue that sexual interaction between adults and children or between older children and younger children is neutral or positive in its impact on a young child (Condy et al, 1987;

Constantine, 1979; Sandfort, 1984; Tindall, 1978). I don't share this opinion. Young children are not mentally, emotionally, or physically mature enough to make an informed choice about whether or not to participate in sexual activities with an adult. Hence, although certain survivors of sexual abuse may identify this experience as positive or neutral in its impact on them, this is certainly not the case for the majority of victims of sexual trauma.

The specific form of expression of the effects of the sexual trauma will vary from individual to individual. It is generally true that while many of the effects of sexual victimization were adaptive responses at the time of victimization, they become dysfunctional in the victims' post-abuse environment (Briere, 1989).

Each person who has been sexually abused has a unique story to tell of how this event has played a part in his life. The remainder of this chapter will describe the various ways that sexual abuse can affect male victims. There is no single classification of impacts that can possibly recognize all the possible outcomes of sexual trauma; however, survivors share many common themes and issues. The primary focus will be on long-term impacts that become integral parts of survivor's lives, rather than on short-term acute impacts.

Remember that your clients' self-reported histories are the most helpful guide to understanding the various impacts of abuse. The information given here is intended to guide you in your understanding of your clients' experience, not to replace a thorough assessment.

Variables That Affect the Impact of Sexual Abuse

Researchers and clinicians have observed that the severity of the impact of sexual abuse on its victims is a function of a number of key variables:

- the age at which the abuse began;
- the duration and frequency of the abuse;
- the type of activities that constituted the abuse;
- the nature of the relationship between the offender and the victim;
- the number and gender of offenders involved in the abuse;
- the manner in which disclosure of the abuse occurred; and
- other attenuating circumstances in the victim's life (Condy

et al., 1987; Crowder & Myers-Avis, 1993; Hunter, 1990a; Pierce, 1987)

The Age at Which the Abuse Began

Generally, the younger a victim at the time the abuse begins, the greater the impact on his psychological development (Hunter, 1990a; Pierce, 1987). Younger children call upon more primitive, less conscious defenses to protect the integrity of their psyche; as the child matures, these primitive defenses often lead to severe developmental impairment (Kilgore, 1988). Defenses such as denial, repression, splitting, and dissociation become problematic if the victim generalizes these coping strategies to a variety of situations in his life. The older a victim is at the time the abuse begins, the more able he is to consciously decide how he will protect himself and fewer developmental stages in his life will be affected by his decisions.

The Duration and Frequency of the Abuse

The more often a victim is abused and the longer the duration of the abuse, the greater the likelihood that he will be conditioned by the experience and, hence, the greater the severity of the impact of the abuse (Hunter, 1990a). The psychological "air" that a child breathes provides the nutrients on which his psyche grows; if this "air" which surrounds him is contaminated, his psyche will be forced to accommodate to this polluted atmosphere. In the same way that pollutants in inner city environments poison children's neurological systems, so does repeated and enduring sexual abuse distort their relationships with self and others.

The Type of Activities Which Constitute the Abuse

The use of force tends to exacerbate the impact of the sexual abuse (Pierce, 1987; Urquiza & Capra, 1990). Threats of violence or acts of violence threaten not only the psychological health of a child but also his physical existence. A child's powerlessness, helplessness, and rage are greater when an offender overpowers him with physical force.

In some cases of ritual abuse, a victim has been forced to be an active participant in abhorrent rituals (such as when he is forced to hold the knife that performs a ritual sacrifice). Often the victim will forget that adults forced or coerced him to comply with their plans and he is overcome with self-blame and self-loathing or represses his cognitive memories of the event. Generally, "In most cases the more deviant the sexual act, the greater the negative impact" (Hunter, 1990a, p. 46).

The Nature of the Relationship Between the Offender and the Victim

Offenders can be complete strangers or the most intimate of family members. Because of the greater intensity of interaction when the offender is a family member or a close friend, the victim's betrayal is also greater. A victim's loyalties to his family members are generally more complex than they are to strangers, so when he is abused by a family member the breach of trust is more highly charged.

Family members often continue to be significant in the victim's life and they are not easily avoided or forgotten; hence, if the abuse is intrafamilial the victim's sense of loss, grief, and betrayal is more severe. A victim who was seduced by a family member who was gentle and kind during the abuse often reports greater difficulty processing his residual feelings than does a victim who was forcefully raped by a stranger.

Seductive abuse strategies utilized by someone with whom the victim had an ongoing relationship create confusion and ambivalence about the nature of the abuse for the victim. Intrafamilial abuse victims generally have mixed loyalties to their abuser(s); their ambivalent feelings of caring for the abuser(s) at the same time as being fearful or enraged about his or her abusive actions can create ongoing patterns of unstable relationships. As Dimock (1988) states:

> [For many male survivors] vulnerability becomes associated with the powerlessness they experienced as a child when someone more powerful took advantage of them. [In adult relationships]...they are unable to separate these past experiences from the present and [they] react emotionally as if they were still powerless when they feel vulnerable. (p. 217)

The Number and Gender of Offenders Involved in the Abuse

"The greater the number of adults who take part in the actual abuse the more likely the child is to form a view of the world as inhabited only by dangerous people" (Hunter, 1990a, p. 48). If, as in ritual abuse, large parts of the child's world revolve around the abuse and its secretive nature, the child comes to believe that there is no other reality. Similarly, if both men and women offend against a child, he feels less safe than if only

one gender abused him. Men who have had multiple perpetrators generally have greater difficulty healing; the dynamics of the abuse are more
complex and the process of recovery is slower.

The Manner in Which Disclosure of the Abuse Occurred

In general, when a victim is able to voluntarily disclose his abuse or
regains his memories of the abuse in a gradual manner, it is less stressful
than if the disclosure is involuntary or abrupt (Kilgore, 1988). If disclosure occurs when a victim is still living at home, the reactions of family
members will be very important. If family members deny or refute the
occurrence of the abuse, the victim's sense of helplessness and hopelessness may be augmented. If, on the other hand, a victim is believed and
supported, his recovery from the sexual trauma is assisted.

A victim's developmental stage influences the manner in which he
discloses his abuse and his abilities to process others' reactions to his
disclosure. Younger children often disclose by reenacting abusive behaviors; adolescents may disclose indirectly by telling a good friend, who, in
turn, tells a trusted authority figure. Adults tend to be more direct in their
disclosure, once they acknowledge their abuse to themselves. In general,
the sooner a victim discloses his abuse and receives treatment for its
negative impacts, the easier his recovery.

It is not uncommon for child victims to retract their abuse disclosures
because the family pressures evoked by the disclosure process are so
horrendous (Summit, 1983). Children are motivated to disclose by desires to have the abusive behavior stop or in order to protect the safety of
another child; they are rarely prepared for the investigation process that
police and child protection agencies are required to conduct or for the
upheaval in the family structure that often results.

Other Attenuating Circumstances in the Victim's Life

Sexual abuse is not the only event that occurs in a child's life. If it is
only a minor occurrence in the midst of other relatively benign experiences, it will have less impact than if it is one part of a potpourri of
physical and emotional abuse and neglect. Three factors that affect a
child's abilities to recover from sexual abuse are:

"(1) the basic constitutional characteristics of the child (for example,
temperament, high self-esteem, and internal locus of control); (2) a
supportive family environment (warmth, nurturance, organization,

and so on); and (3) a supportive individual or agency that provides a primary support system to assist the child in coping and in developing a positive model for identification. (Urquiza & Capra, 1990, p. 129)

Effects of Sexual Abuse on Male Survivors

Sexual abuse is a multilayered assault that is often accompanied by other forms of abuse and neglect. Therefore, to isolate single symptoms or to overlook the interrelated nature of the symptoms that result from sexual abuse is to present an inaccurate picture of most survivors' experience.

This text examines the impacts of sexual abuse on male victims from a clinical viewpoint. General post-abuse symptoms are examined before more complex abuse-specific symptoms, such as dissociation, are reviewed. I will discuss the typical effects of sexual abuse on males under the following headings:

- physical impacts;
- mental impacts;
- emotional impacts;
- Posttraumatic Stress Disorder (PTSD) and dissociation;
- difficulties with male gender identity;
- sexual orientation confusion and homophobia;
- abuse-reactive perpetration and aggression;
- sexual compulsions and addictions; and
- interpersonal difficulties.

Physical Impacts

Children generally lack a vocabulary to tell others of their abuse experiences or to describe the impact of those experiences on them. They will tend to "show" others their experience, by reenacting it or by other behavioral indicators. It is quite common for boys who have been abused to have nightmares and sleep disturbances, to be encopretic or enuretic, or to display other physical symptoms of distress (Urquiza & Capra, 1990). Chronic somatic complaints for which there are no apparent organic cause can be indicators of abuse.

Some victims develop disgust and self-hatred for their physical selves. (Hunter, 1990; Myers, 1989). Boys often feel betrayed by their bodies.

which have responded to the perpetrators' sexual overtures; their internal feelings of confusion or fear or anger were in conflict with their physical arousal. This contempt for the physical self manifests in a variety of ways, such as neglecting one's physical needs (e.g., over- or undereating, not attending to medical needs) or self-abuse.

Self-abusive behaviors can take a variety of forms—a readiness to take unsafe physical risks (e.g., reckless driving, unsafe sexual practices, etc.), alcohol or drug addictions, active self-mutilation are some of the more common ones. Self-mutilation is often "an attempt to block or interrupt negative cognitions or feelings…and thus may be an attempt to survive incapacitating symptoms…." (Briere, 1989, p. 27). It is not uncommon for survivors to display their self-hatred and despair in suicidal ideation or in actual suicide attempts (Dixon, Arnold, & Calestro, 1978; McCormack, Janus, & Burgess, 1986).

Self-harming behaviors can indicate a variety of different dynamics and you must examine each client's personal beliefs in order to understand the metaphoric significance of his behavior. For example, with clients who have Multiple Personality Disorder (MPD), self-harming behavior may be the domain of a particular personality; unless you work with that specific personality, the client may not be able to access the emotions that fuel the self-harming actions.

When sexuality has been the way to meet a variety of nonsexual needs, a survivor may view his body and his sexuality as commodities to trade for money or lodging. Such behavior may become part of a survivor's lifestyle. Male prostitutes and male runaways who learned as child victims of sexual abuse that their sexuality can be a means of gaining power and resources resort to using their bodies as a means of obtaining a livelihood (McCormack, Janus, & Burgess, 1986).

To be a male victim is a countercultural experience since men are not generally seen as vulnerable and powerless. Some male victims fear that their vulnerability is transparent and that even perfect strangers can see they have been victimized and are therefore flawed. Sometimes they become involved in counterphobic activities such as bodybuilding and athletic activities, not for a love of sport, but as a way of becoming more powerful and hiding their "weaknesses."

Mental Impacts

One of the most common cognitive distortions displayed by survivors is that they hold themselves responsible for having been abused (Briere et al., 1988; McCormack, Janus, & Burgess, 1986; Myers, 1989; Nielsen,

1983; Vander May, 1988). Children have a limited understanding of the interpersonal dynamics in which they participate. When they are abused or neglected, they understand this as being the result of inadequacies in themselves, rather than as the result of inadequacies in the adults who are abusing or neglecting them (Leehan & Wilson, 1985). This tendency to self-blame is often exacerbated by the abuser, who may say, "You made me do this...," or "I'm doing this because I love you...," or "If you weren't so sexy, I wouldn't have to do this...."

Many survivors, as adults, need assistance in understanding that a child is not responsible for the behavior of an adult, under any circumstances. Survivors often look back on their abuse history and project adult values and judgements onto their own involvement in the experience; they forget that as children they were not sufficiently mentally or emotionally mature to make decisions about the ethics of their sexual behavior. Helping a survivor to see himself as the child that he was at the time of the abuse can often reduce his sense of having been responsible for it.

Survivors commonly repress abuse-related memories or deny the impact of having been abused (Briere, 1989). Usually, they developed these mental defenses at the time of the abuse in an attempt to cope with the dissonant events in their lives. For instance, in cases of intrafamilial abuse, many child victims were placed in the dilemma of being abused by people who also expressed love and caring towards them. Trying to understand this discordant behavior, the child may have found that by denying or unconsciously repressing his abuse memories he could tolerate his life situation.

Survivors often exhibit patterns of learned helplessness and passivity (Blanchard, 1986; Briere, 1989).

> Although the victim mentality begins as a useful childhood coping mechanism, when it continues into adulthood, it becomes obsolete. The victimized person has become an adult, with the choices and power of a man, but he continues to think of himself as little, helpless and at fault for all the mistreatment he receives. He goes through his adult life training others to treat him poorly by being passive and not standing up for himself.... The abuse was a normal part of his childhood and nobody did anything to stop it, so he thinks that abuse is a normal, acceptable part of life. (Hunter, 1990a pp. 71–72)

Survivors who believe they were responsible for their abuse and can do nothing to change their life experience often have very low self-esteem

(Nielsen, 1983). They believe that the treatment they received from adults was what they deserved and the world has nothing better to offer them. This hopelessness and helplessness can become a self-fulfilling prophecy if the survivor does not find a way to change these inner beliefs.

Emotional Impacts

Men in our culture have, until recently, received little support for the outward expression of their feelings. Survivors have often been encouraged by their socialization to suppress or repress their affect. Many male survivors are unable to identify, acknowledge, or disclose their feelings; they experience affective numbness (Hunter, 1990a; Leehan & Wilson, 1985). Some homophobic men believe that only homosexual men express emotion and they develop a stoic persona to confirm their "masculinity."

Some men are unaware of their emotions and they develop addictive behaviors to ensure that these emotions are suppressed (Urquiza & Capra, 1990). Addictions are unconscious secondary emotional processes that temporarily block out primary affect. The compulsive nature of addictive behavior is so engrossing and temporarily satisfying that it masks the deeper emotional reality that underlies it.

Many survivors exhibit substance addictions and their relationship to alcohol, drugs, or food can consume much of their mental and emotional energy. Other survivors develop process addictions and their relationships with work, sports, sex, or other endeavors exhibit obsessive and addictive patterns. In this way, their work or their interest in sports becomes all-consuming because it takes on the secondary function of acting as a barrier to emotional processing. Process addictions are often socially well received and may earn a survivor the respect of his boss or his teammates. It is not generally apparent to the people who benefit from the survivor's process addictions that his activity is, in fact, driven by a need to block emotional awareness.

When a survivor is in touch with his emotions, he is likely to experience feelings of anxiety and fear, depression, guilt, anger and rage, and shame (Blanchard, 1986; Briere, 1989; Bruckner & Johnson, 1987; Constantine, 1979; Hunter, 1990a; Nielsen, 1983; Olsen, 1990; Pierce, 1987; Schacht, Kerlinsky, & Carlson, 1990; Urquiza & Capra, 1990; Vander May, 1988).

Initially, anger is the emotion that survivors often feel most comfortable expressing (Dimock, 1988). Men's rage is often connected to the homosexuality of the abuse, rather than to its exploitive aspects. Anger is powerful and energy-filled and it is an affective state that is egosyntonic with masculine cultural roles. Anger and rage can become a "catchall" emotion for male victims. Because it is a powerful and active emotion, expressing anger feels more acceptable than displaying more vulnerable emotions.

However, not all male survivors experience anger at having been abused. Many have difficulty accessing and expressing their rage. For many men, anger is associated with violence. Many survivors are afraid that if they contact their angry feelings they will express them violently. Other survivors adopt a "victim" stance in their lives and respond with passivity and withdrawal to having been exploited.

Post Traumatic Stress Disorder (PTSD) and Dissociation

People working in the rape-crisis area, the Vietnam War veterans area, and the child sexual abuse area have pooled their knowledge to create an understanding of the effects of severe trauma on its victims. This combined knowledge has become known as the study of posttraumatic stress. It has provided very helpful conceptualizations for those who work with survivors of natural disasters, wars, hostage-takings, rape, and, most recently, sexual abuse.

Victims of sexual abuse share many issues in common with victims of other disasters. These include:

- they didn't choose the frequency or duration of the traumatic event;
- their personal resources are overwhelmed by powerful, negative forces;
- their physical and psychological safety was threatened;
- they didn't know when their environment was safe and when it wasn't;
- their efforts to talk about the trauma with others are often met with incredulity and insufficient understanding, which results in emotional isolation, confusion, and shame; and
- they're unable to process the trauma emotionally until they feel physically and psychologically safe. (Briere, 1989; Evans, 1990)

The etiological features of Post Traumatic Stress Disorder (PTSD) provoke a variety of coping strategies by which a victim attempts to preserve his integrity. The most common PTSD symptoms include flashbacks and reexperiencing the trauma (Briere, 1989), a general numbing of mental and affective responsiveness (Blanchard, 1986; Briere, 1989; Myers, 1989), hypervigilance (Blanchard, 1986; Briere, 1989), and a variety of dissociative responses (Briere, 1989; Evans, 1990; Hunter, 1990a; Nielsen, 1983).

Flashbacks can involve any or all of a survivor's five senses which have either consciously or unconsciously encoded memory of the abuse (Briere, 1989). Often, survivors report vague recurrent body sensations for which they have no conscious cognitive memory. These sensations or memories occur when the survivor is triggered by either internal or external stimuli that evoke the original trauma. For instance, a survivor whose abuse included posing for pornographic pictures may experience a flashback triggered by the appearance of a camera; or a survivor who was left alone for long periods of time after having been abused may flash back to the abuse experience when he feels isolated or lonely.

The more often a trauma has been repeated and the more intrusive its nature, the deeper and stronger the survivor's neurological memory of the event. If a trigger event occurs in the survivor's current life that recalls previous abusive events, a chain of associations occurs, usually unconsciously, and the client begins to reexperience the abuse incident. This reexperiencing will often involve a blurring between past and present; the survivor unconsciously withdraws from the present and projects past memories and feelings onto here-and-now stimuli. This trance-like event is accompanied by decreased sensory awareness and the survivor generally needs to reconnect with his present reality in order to move through the flashback.

Repressed memories can return as flashbacks; they can also emerge in the form of dreams and nightmares. Survivors commonly have dreams that explicitly recall their abuse or they experience recurrent nightmares of being pursued that symbolically evoke themes of abuse (Briere, 1989; Nielsen, 1983).

Briere (1989) defines the common PTSD symptom of *emotional numbing* as "…a loss of reactivity, detachment from others and/or constricted emotionality" (p. 8). Male survivors often report explicit details of their abuse without any emotionality, as if they were talking about events that had happened to someone else. Although emotional distancing has a short-term value as a means of coping with shock and crisis, if it is sustained over a long period of time, it separates and isolates the survivor from his full range of feelings (Grubman-Black, 1990; Nielsen, 1983). It is quite common for survivors to be afraid of identifying or expressing their feelings because they fear that their affective responses will be so intense that they won't be able to manage them.

Often survivors of trauma and sexual abuse become *hypervigilant,* keeping themselves prepared for the next potential assault on their personhood (Blanchard, 1986). PTSD is typified by hypertension and the overactivity of the sympathetic nervous system. Chronic muscle tension; an inability to sleep or restless, disturbed sleeping patterns; and exaggerated startle responses are typical symptoms displayed by survivors of sexual trauma (Nielsen, 1983).

A common reaction to trauma, and to sexual abuse in particular, is that the victim dissociates from the experience. A child's body may remain present during the abuse activities, but his mind and spirit separate themselves as a means of psychological self-protection. Some of the symptoms of *dissociation* that Briere (1989) notes are cognitive disengagement into seemingly neutral space (better known as "spacing out"), derealization (the feeling that things around you are false or unreal), depersonalization (feeling that you are different from your usual self), out-of-body experiences (the sensation of floating outside your body and travelling elsewhere), and circumscribed blanks in otherwise continuous memory (Briere, 1989, p. 7).

Dissociative behaviors fall on a continuum from daydreaming to Multiple Personality Disorder (MPD). Mild forms of dissociation are common everyday experiences. However, when more extreme dissociative defenses, such as splitting and repression, are used to cope with stressors, they interfere with a sense of personal integrity.

Many survivors have dissociated their affect from their cognitive memory. Others have a vague, uneasy feeling that they were abused, but they cannot recollect specific abusive events. In either case, the survivor often feels crazy and partialized. Therapy has the task of helping him to reintegrate the full spectrum of his experience.

When a victim is abused at a young age and the abuse is severe and prolonged and has involved several different offenders, it is not uncommon for a victim to develop highly dissociative defenses, such as Multiple Personality Disorder (MPD). MPD is a sophisticated unconscious defense in which the psyche paradoxically attempts to protect its coherence by partializing its various components. Subpersonalities serve the MPD system by taking on the tasks of protectors, aggressors, or victims. Generally, the subpersonalities are very distinct from one another, with very different traits and characteristics. Memories held by each subpersonality are not shared with the other parts of the system; hence, survivors with MPD often have apparent memory loss or have been told by others about actions they did but don't remember doing.

Difficulties with Male Gender Identity

Our culture has created a social mythology that expects men to be in control, self-sufficient, and powerful. Men are not supposed to need assistance in coping with their feelings. Expressions such as "Big boys don't cry" encourage males to hide their vulnerability. Successful men in our culture are portrayed as heterosexual, as sexual initiators, and as protectors of themselves and others.

For male survivors, the social prescription for successful manhood directly conflicts with their experience. Often, survivors rewrite their abuse history, forgetting that they were powerless children at the time. They project their mature identities onto their memories of the abuse and hold themselves responsible for not having stopped their offender from abusing them. As a result of abuse, many men report "...damage to their subjective sense of maleness or masculinity..." (Myers, 1989, p. 210).

Certain social attitudes increase a male survivor's alienation from a healthy masculine gender identity; when a survivor's disclosure of abuse is met with questions such as "Are you an offender?" or "Are you gay?" his sense of being flawed is confirmed (Dimock, 1988; Myers, 1989). Prevalent among survivors is the feeling:

> that they responded sexually in circumstances in which a normal man would have been impotent. As a result, they came to regard themselves as abnormal, which in turn kindled or rekindled feelings of inadequacy as a man. (Sarrel & Masters, 1982, p. 127)

In the course of therapy, male survivors need to examine how their ability to claim their own authentic masculinity is limited by cultural factors. Grubman-Black (1990) says therapists can help clients develop a positive masculine gender identity by recognizing that rigid ideas about gender roles and stereotypes based on inadequate information are responsible for some of a survivor's personal suffering in the aftermath of abuse. Therapists can help victims to be aware that today there are new and emerging definitions of masculinity that are affirmative and positive, often based on a humanist or feminist position.

Sexual Orientation Confusion and Homophobia

Many male survivors have been abused by a male offender and this inevitably raises questions for the survivor about his sexual orientation and masculinity. He may be confused about whether his natural sexual orientation is heterosexual, homosexual, or bisexual (Bruckner & Johnson, 1987; Dimock, 1988; Hunter, 1990a; Myers, 1989). Questions and concerns about sexual orientation are often a core issue for male survivors. They may express confusion about their natural sexual inclination: Dimock (1988) observes that many survivors engage in sexual activity with a partner of the sex opposite to their stated sexual orientation or are unable to state their sexual preference.

Generally, victims have been physiologically aroused by the offender's stimulation of their genitals. Often, the sexual abuse is a victim's first orgasmic experience with another person. In attempting to understand their experience, many victims will use external cues (i.e., physical arousal and orgasm) rather than internal cues (i.e., emotional discomfort and confusion) in their attempts to identify sexual preference and orientation. They develop a belief that "...arousal equals pleasure and pleasure equals complicity" (Gerber, 1990, p. 173).

Children are not aware that many men who engage in same-sex behaviors are not homosexual. They do not analyze their experience in relation to power and control issues. Often a child will have understood his experience of being abused as a homosexual experience rather than as an abusive experience. He will see the perpetrator as being "a gay man who was being sexual with a child" rather than as "a child molester who was sexually using a child to meet primarily nonsexual needs."

All survivors ask the questions, "Why did this happen to me and not to someone else?" "What does having been sexually abused say about me and my sexuality?" and "Why was I chosen?" For survivors who were abused by a same-sex offender there are further questions. Homosexual men will tend to ask themselves "Am I gay because of having been abused?" or "Was I abused because I am gay?" Heterosexual men will wonder, "If I was abused by a man, does this mean that I am really gay?"

Our society is very homophobic. Both heterosexual and homosexual men who have grown up in this culture have internalized homophobic beliefs. For gay men, the "coming out" process can be more difficult if they are survivors of sexual abuse because of their own uncertainty about the impact of the abuse on their sexual orientation. Their families and friends may discount their sexual orientation and dismiss it by saying,

"He's gay because he was sexually abused." Their own internalized homophobia may encourage them to see their abuse as having determined their sexual orientation, because they can then believe that recovery from the abuse will include a "cure" for being gay.

At the present time, there is no predictable relationship between sexual orientation and childhood sexual abuse. Some researchers have shown "a statistically strong...relationship between childhood sexual abuse and homosexual activity in adulthood" (Dimock, 1988, p. 205), but whether this demonstrates cause, effect, or correlation is unknown.

There is some evidence that boys who are marginalized are more vulnerable to being abused (Finkelhor, 1984). To the extent that boys who depart from traditional masculine gender-bound identities (i.e., boys who don't like sports, who are feeling-oriented, etc.) are more marginalized, they may be more likely to be abused. Research into this aspect of abuse is fraught with political and ethical concerns and the researcher runs the risk of being seen as anti-gay and homophobic (Hunter, 1990a).

Clearly, therapists (be they male, female, homosexual, or heterosexual) have an obligation to become aware of their own biases regarding sexism, racism, classism, and sexual orientation. While we are aware that sexual orientation ranges from heterosexuality through bisexuality to homosexuality, our knowledge and understanding about these choices tend to gravitate towards the poles of heterosexuality and homosexuality. How the continuum between these two poles is affected by innate, situational, or transitional variables is not well understood. Clinicians need to encourage further research into the interface between sexual abuse and subsequent sexual identity.

Therapists must ensure that their clients' interests, not their own, are served by the balance between therapeutic and political concerns that occurs in therapy sessions. To optimize the usefulness of the therapeutic process for clients, therapists need to become consciously aware of their own cultural and political biases and how these affect their interventions with clients.

Abuse-Reactive Perpetration and Aggression

Victims appear to have three typical unconscious responses to the experience of sexual victimization.

1. The child knows what it feels like to be a victim and unconsciously decides, "This is who I am." He accepts

his victimization experience as a reflection of his self-worth, never defines his boundaries and limits, and is repeatedly revictimized.

2. The child knows what it feels like to be a victim,and unconsciously decides, "I'll protect others from ever becoming victims." He pursues this belief by giving others the help and protection he never received himself.

3. The child knows what it feels like to be a victim and unconsciously decides, "I'll never be a victim again." His way of regaining power is to identify with the aggressor and use abusive strategies to meet his needs.

Although male survivors can adopt more than one of these responses, identification with one position usually predominates. Many survivors, even if their primary identification is as a victim or protector, worry that they will also become a perpetrator. Bruckner and Johnson (1987) point out that it's quite common for survivors to feel afraid of becoming sexual with children or to feel guilty for having had sexual experiences with children when they were adolescents.

Obviously, not all victims become sexual offenders and not all sexual offenders were victims of sexual abuse. Certain factors lessen the likelihood that a victim will become a victimizer. Having a strong sense of self prior to the abuse experience, having a relationship with positive male role models, having supportive interpersonal relationships, and developing an awareness of healthy sexual expression are some of the factors that reduce the likelihood of a victim becoming an offender (Gerber, 1990).

Some victims of abuse unconsciously internalize the behavior of their offender. Social learning theory suggests that modelling and vicarious learning play a large part in how social behaviors are shaped and expressed. For some victims, acting abusively becomes a defense against being a victim, since they believe that it is better to be powerful than weak and that you need to control others to be powerful. This identification with the aggressor may lead some survivors to acts of abuse against others as a maladaptive means of meeting their needs to be powerful (Gerber, 1990). It may represent a misguided counterphobic attempt to understand and gain mastery over their victimization experience (Hunter, 1990a).

Male socialization encourages action and tolerates aggression in ensuring need gratification. For some survivors, their limited repertoire of skills to meet their needs results in using controlling and manipulative behaviors with others. Bruckner and Johnson (1987) note that members of male survivor groups often admit to sexual aggression with adult partners, to physical assault of partners, and to general manipulation of relationships.

When survivors have themselves perpetrated against others, a thorough assessment is needed to ascertain whether this behavior is a patterned, predatory, deliberate grooming process or whether it is an isolated abuse-reactive experience resulting from behaviorial experimentation or behavior replication. It is not within the scope of this text to address the assessment and treatment for repeat sexual offenders. However, given that some survivors will have engaged in abuse-reactive perpetration, some issues associated with offending behavior will be discussed.

Often survivors who have engaged in abuse-reactive sexual activity as adolescents feel greatly ashamed of this behavior. This double-layered shame, about being both a victim and a victimizer, must be addressed. Survivors often need to have their offending behavior contextualized vis-à-vis their own victimization. This is not an attempt to excuse this behavior, but rather a strategy to reduce the client's shame about it. Reducing the level of shame empowers the client to move into feeling appropriately guilty and taking responsibility for having offended, thus becoming accountable for his behavior.

Survivors need to know that a child who has been prematurely sexually awakened has his sexual energy operating without adequate judgement and maturity. As he matures, a survivor will have to examine his early sexual experience and possibly correct some unconscious dysfunctional patterns. The survivor's need to be powerful and to express his rage at having been victimized will have to be channelled into nonabusive behaviors.

Survivors who are both victims and victimizers present a challenge to many mental health professionals. Therapists are often confronted with the limitations of their fondly held theories about victims and offenders (Gerber, 1990). When the boundary between "victim" and "offender" is blurred, models of treatment that focus exclusively on victimization or on offending processes as discrete events are no longer as useful. Many agencies separate services to victims and offenders; clients who fit both categories create a service delivery dilemma.

Sexual Addictions and Compulsions

Sexual behavior has a strong inherent reinforcer—namely, sexual arousal and orgasm. Victims' sexual arousal patterns are conditioned by sexual abuse; by definition, sexual abuse creates dysfunctional conditioning. Since young children do not have the emotional, cognitive, or social orientation with which to make meaning of adult sexual experience, their abusive sexual initiation can establish patterns of arousal and sexualized coping behaviors that can be dysfunctional in later developmental stages. Friedrich, Beilke, and Urquiza (1988) compared the behavior of two groups of young boys aged three to eight years of age. One group was conduct disordered and the other was sexually abused. They found that they could discriminate who was in which group with a relatively high degree of accuracy. The variable that contributed most to this discrimination was sex problems. The sexually abused boys were significantly more sexualized as a group. The sexual behavior of these young boys included excessive masturbation, a preoccupation with sex, and reenacting their abuse with siblings. Unless victims such as these young boys receive abuse-focused counselling at the time of disclosure, their sexual expression will develop in ways that reflect their initial abusive sexual experience.

For males in our culture, the first orgasm is a rite of passage and signifies entry into manhood. When this orgasm occurs in the context of an abusive interaction, it is imbued with problematic associations such as coercion, nonmutual exchange, and sometimes violence. Some survivors build masturbatory fantasies and rituals around the experience of their abuse and are aroused by aggressive, violent, or exploitative sexual activities.

The pairing of secrecy and sexual arousal often leaves a victim feeling very ashamed of his sexuality, especially if he senses that his sexual expression is deviant. Some survivors are unaware that their sexual behavior has been shaped by abuse processes and they believe that they are misfits or weird or crazy because of the nature of their sexual desires and expression.

There is often an analogous pattern between a victim's abuse experience and his subsequent sexual expression. For instance, if the abuse experience involved acts of violence and sadism, the victim's subsequent sexual expression may well replicate aspects of this violence. Because of the shame surrounding this behavior, a survivor will generally be very reluctant to let others know about this aspect of his sexuality.

Many survivors report compulsive sexual behaviors such as frequent nonrelational sexual activities with others or compulsive masturbation.

Compulsive sexual behavior may be simply defined as a lack of control over one or more specific sexual activities. Such activities are most often ego-alien and the individual feels shame and remorse after engaging in such behaviours. In spite of a desire to stop, he is unable to, even when it's clear that he may be causing himself or others harm. (Dimock, 1988, p. 207)

Like other addictions, sexual addictions are usually a misguided attempt on the part of the survivor to self-medicate. Compulsive sexual behaviors are used to block states of mind (e.g. anxiety) that are intolerable to the survivor. For some survivors, sexual addictions are used to replace sexual intimacy. Masturbating with pornographic material is less threatening than having to relate sexually with a partner, especially since interactive sexual situations will often bring back memories of the abuse, either consciously or unconsciously (Hunter, 1990a). In some cases, survivors attempt to manage their sexual discomfort by completely avoiding sexual contact with others (Bruckner & Johnson, 1987).

In order for the client to be able to change his addictive behavior, he needs to become aware of his addictive cycle. Becoming familiar with the sequencing of his compulsive behavior and the states of mind that precede his addictive behavior helps a survivor to decode his compulsive actions and to develop functional behavioral substitutes.

Interpersonal Difficulties

Sexual abuse is a human-induced trauma and it has long-lasting repercussions on subsequent human relationships. In young children, abuse-related reactions include aggression towards others, delinquency, and non-compliance (McCormack, Janus, & Burgess, 1986; Schacht, Kerlinsky, & Carlson, 1990; Urquiza & Capra, 1990). Often victims of abuse have mixed loyalties to the abuser; although they may have disliked the one-sided aspect of the sexual relationship, they may have liked the perpetrator's attention and interest (Blanchard, 1986; Hunter, 1990a; Nielsen, 1893). These mixed loyalties can later manifest as an inability to distinguish between sexuality and affection, trust and exploitation, and safe or abusive relationships (Briere, 1989).

Victims of abuse can experience difficulty in initiating, developing, and maintaining close interpersonal intimate relationships (Urquiza & Capra, 1990). Often, the betrayal of trust that is inherent in sexual abuse leads the victim to withdraw from interpersonal relationships. This social isolation exaggerates the victim's stigmatization and leaves him less able to successfully integrate the psychosocial crisis of abuse (Briere, 1989; Leehan & Wilson, 1985).

Researchers and clinicians have noted that survivors of sexual abuse are more likely to be revictimized in subsequent relationships (Briere, 1989; Dimock, 1988; Hunter, 1990a; Myers, 1989; Nielsen, 1983). The dynamics of this revictimization process are complex. Some victims are not well attuned to the danger signals that indicate potentially abusive situations: either they dissociate in the face of them, entering a passive ego state in which their abilities to protect themselves are absent, or these signals are so much part of their normal experience that they can't imagine nonabusive interpersonal interactions. Other victims have difficulty discerning their personal boundaries and limits and are unable to identify the times when their needs for safety are not being met.

One reaction to childhood victimization is that victims become hypervigilant to the moods and behaviors of other significant people in their environment (Blanchard, 1986; Briere, 1989). As a child, attempting to predict when an abusive event was likely to occur gave the child a marginal sense of control. Learning to read the abuser's state of mind and moods was an integral part of developing this false sense of control. This initially safety-based behavior becomes dysfunctional in later adult relationships when a survivor cannot identify his own internal experience and is focused on the internal state of the significant others in his life. His sense of self worth becomes distorted and his own behavior is shaped in reaction to others rather than in response to his own needs.

Survivors' interactive sexual behavior is often very problematic (Blanchard, 1986; Briere, 1989; Myers, 1989; Nielsen, 1983; Sarrel & Masters, 1982). A variety of sexual dysfunctions such as a lack of desire, erectile problems, or dissociation during sexual activities, can haunt a survivor.

Sexual abuse generally accelerates, retards, or convolutes a child's sexual development. As an abuse victim matures, his psychosexual development will reflect his abuse-related experience. In adult relationships, sexual partners will sometimes carry the survivor's unconscious projections from his abuse experience and this can be confusing and distressing for both people until such time as these problems can be identified and addressed. For example, if the offender rewarded the victim with post-abuse gifts, as an adult the victim may be very negatively reactive to any gifts he received from his lovers. This may be confusing for his lover who expects his gifts to produce enjoyment and also for the survivor who cannot understand his own response to his lover's behavior.

DIFFERENCES BETWEEN MALE AND FEMALE SURVIVORS OF SEXUAL ABUSE

Current research indicates that there are some significant differences between the sexual victimization of boys and girls. These differences exist both in the nature of the abuse experience itself and in how this experience is understood and integrated.

Information about the differences between male and female survivors will be presented in the following manner: First, I will discuss the research findings about these differences; second, I will describe some of the contributors' observations about the ways client gender affects the therapeutic process.

Determining the prevalence rates of the sexual victimization of boys and girls is fraught with complexities. Current research studies indicate that in absolute numbers more girls than boys are sexually abused (Bruckner & Johnson, 1987; Finklehor, 1984; Fritz, Stoll, & Wagner, 1981; Vander May, 1988). It remains to be seen whether these findings will change as social conditions permit men to acknowledge their victimization experiences.

Research findings consistently note that boys and girls experience sexual abuse differently. Males often frame sexual abuse as a sexual initiation, rather than as a violation of their personhood (Condy et al., 1987; Constantine, 1979; Finklehor, 1984; Fritz, Stoll, & Wagner, 1981; Risin & Koss, 1987; Sandfort, 1984; Tindall, 1978). According to Fritz, Stoll, and Wagner (1981), females tended to assign a decidedly harmful, negative quality to their prepubescent sexual experience, while males were neutral or even positive about it.

The difference in victims' perceptions of their sexual abuse is shaped by many factors, including gender socialization, the different physiological responses of the sexes, and culturally determined expressions of sexuality. Although male victims may not perceive their abuse as negative, this does not mean that they weren't negatively affected. As Finklehor (1984) discovered in his investigation of male survivors, boys were more likely than girls to cite interest and pleasure as their immediate reaction to being sexually abused. However, when he looked at the long-term effects of abuse as measured by its impact on sexual self-esteem, Finklehor noted that the boys were affected as much as, if not more than, the girls.

Male victims are more often homosexually abused than female victims (Finklehor, 1984; Fritz, Stoll, & Wagner, 1981; Risin & Koss, 1987). The reality of victimization is that boys, like girls, are most commonly victimized by men.

Researchers have found that female victims are more often abused by family members, while boys are more frequently the victims of extrafamilial abusers (Finklehor, 1984; Fritz, Stoll, & Wagner, 1981; Pierce & Pierce, 1985; Risin & Koss, 1987; Vander May, 1988). Statistically, boys are at greater risk of being abused by teachers, coaches, babysitters, and other adult authority figures than by members of their own family. However, empirical research shows that the absolute number of boys who are sexually abused within the family is still very high.

Male victims live in single-parent, mother-headed households more frequently than do female victims (Pierce & Pierce, 1985; Vander May, 1988). Many male victims lack an active male parent or nurturing, protective male model.

It is more common for boys to be abused in conjunction with other children; girls are more likely to be sexually abused in isolation. In cases where the abuse is intrafamilial, the chances of a boy being one of several victims are greater (Dixon, Arnold, & Calestro, 1978; Finklehor, 1984; Fritz, Stoll, & Wagner, 1981; Pierce & Pierce, 1985; Vander May, 1988).

If a girl is abused by a parent, in 65% of the reports she will be the only reported victim. If a boy is abused, 60% of the time there will be another victim. (Finklehor, 1984, p. 164)

Boys who are sexually abused are also more likely to be physically abused than girls (Dixon, Arnold, & Calestro, 1978; Finklehor, 1984; Vander May, 1988). Not only are male sexual abuse victims at greater risk of being physically abused, it is also more likely that their sexual abuse will be violent. Pierce and Pierce (1985) found that the use of force and threats occurred significantly more often with boys than with girls.

The types of activities that constitute abuse differ between male and female victims (Pierce & Pierce, 1985; Risin & Koss, 1987). Male victims are much more frequently the victims of sodomy and are more frequently participants in mutual masturbation. In addition, male victims experience orgasm more frequently during the abuse experience (Fritz, Stoll, & Wagner, 1978). One research study conducted by Pierce and Pierce (1985) found that perpetrators engaged in oral intercourse more often with boys (52% of the boys and 17% of the girls were engaged in oral sex). The same study found that 40% of the perpetrators masturbated the male victim, which is also higher than for females. Boys were fondled much less frequently than girls.

Male victims are less likely to talk about their victimization experiences with family members than are female victims (Fritz, Stoll, & Wagner, 1978; Risin & Koss, 1987). Upon disclosure of the abuse, if the male victim is still a juvenile, his abuse is more likely to be reported to the police than to a child protection agency; if it is reported to protective services, the male victim is less likely to be placed in protective custody (Finklehor, 1984; Pierce & Pierce, 1985; Vander May, 1988). After disclosure, male victims are less likely to receive counselling than female victims; when they do, the average length of treatment is shorter (Vander May, 1988).

The clinicians interviewed for this book were quick to point out that the differences between male and female victims of sexual abuse are few compared to the similarities. Both male and female victims of sexual trauma feel isolated and marginalized. Both struggle with low self-esteem and a damaged sense of self. Ultimately, healing and recovery for both male and female victims involve embracing all aspects of one's humanity, a process that goes beyond gender.

A difference between the genders that contributors frequently commented upon is the reluctance that male victims display about acknowledging their victimization. Men have greater shame attached to their victimization than women do; being a victim is a countercultural experience for a man. Admitting to having been victimized, to having been a powerless child, is more difficult for men. Some men completely refuse to open the door to their memories and feelings, saying, "My childhood experience is in the past."

This difficulty in breaking silence and disclosing abuse-related history to others results in fewer men than women seeking professional assistance to help them to heal from their traumatic experiences. When men do come into therapy, fewer of them identify their history of having been abused as a presenting problem. Many victims of abuse seek counselling for relationship problems or sexual problems and they have not made a cognitive connection between their present problems and their victimization history.

Contributors have observed that male survivors tend to identify sexual concerns (i.e., sexual dysfunctions, sexual orientation issues, or gender identity issues) as presenting issues more frequently than female survivors. Women survivors also have sexuality issues, but these are infrequently their dominant presenting concerns; when these issues surface during the course of therapy, they have a different focus than male victims' sexual concerns.

It is suggested that our culture encourages men to use sexuality, particularly their genitally focused sexuality, as a primary component of self-identity; hence, when this aspect of a man's life is not functioning well, he struggles with an impaired sense of self. Women are encouraged to identify with their relationships; for women, sexuality is only one part of other intimate behavior. Hence, women are focused less on their sexuality and more on the quality of their intimate relationships.

The cultural script that supports women in knowing themselves through their relationships with others and encourages men to be more self-sufficient has other implications for abuse survivors. Bruckner and Johnson (1987), whose experience includes providing group treatment to both male and female survivors, note that the men tend not to associate with each other outside the group, whereas the female participants frequently form relationships. Since isolation is a key issue for male survivors, encouraging them to risk creating relationships with others, including fellow group members, can be a critical step in their healing process.

The now common catch-phrase "men act out; women act in" applies to sexual abuse survivors. Contributors remarked that women survivors show a greater tendency to be depressed and to engage in self-harming behaviors, whereas male survivors tend to express their anger at the abuser and exhibit aggressive tendencies toward others. Many male survivors sublimate their anger at having been abused into generalized antisocial behaviour.

In therapy, male survivors tend to be able to contact their anger and rage at having been abused long before they can feel their grief. They often display active and violent revenge fantasies. Women survivors, on the other hand, are initially more in touch with their sadness and depression; their rage at having been victimized usually surfaces later in the therapeutic process.

In answer to the question "Do you detect differences in the dissociation process between male and female survivors?" contributors gave a variety of responses. Some said they could see no difference. Others, however, suggested that their male clients are more dissociated from the affective components of their abuse, while their female clients are more dissociated from the cognitive components of their abuse.

Male survivors often tell the story of their abuse quite matter-of-factly, describing in detail the behaviors involved in the abuse. However, they talk about these events as if they had happened to someone else, expressing little affect or compassion. Female survivors generally have more difficulty recalling the specific events that comprised the abuse and more difficulty telling others about it. However, they experience intense feelings related to these events, whether or not they can accurately recall them.

Therapists who have offered abuse-focused group treatment to both genders note that the men were more action-oriented than the women. Because of this readiness to take action, therapists need to ensure that their male sexual abuse clients are emotionally prepared for any behaviors they are planning to undertake. Premature confrontation of an abuser or ill-conceived acts of angry revenge can be countertherapeutic.

Chapter 3

Treatment Model and Stages of Healing

This chapter presents information about the basic tenets of therapy with male survivors. It develops a treatment model that is based on principles of partnership between the client and therapist and that supports the client's innate abilities to recover from sexual abuse. The model describes four phases of healing, namely, Breaking Silence, the Victim Phase, the Survivor Phase, and the Thriver Phase. This four-phase model is used as a framework for presenting specific therapeutic interventions in subsequent chapters.

The isomorphic similarity between sexual abuse and therapy was discussed in the introductory section of this text. Abuse processes occur over time, in a relationship in which the offender's needs are given priority over the victim's needs. The abuse-related activities are kept a secret because of the shame that surrounds them. The therapeutic process has the potential to replicate these elements of abuse and to itself become an abusive process. If the therapy is designed to meet the therapist's needs and not the client's and if the confidentiality of the process is used to protect the therapist rather than the client, it can become a counterproductive experience for the client. The client's belief that people will attempt to use him for their own ends and that safe, intimate relationships are not possible, at least for him, will be reinforced.

However, in a manner that echoes the principles of homeopathic medicine, therapy, because of its structural similarities to the abuse process, can also heal the wounds caused by abuse. When a client can proceed

41

through his therapeutic journey with support to reclaim his own power, therapy can be an effective tool for recovery. Successful therapy will allow clients to experience respectful and nonexploitative power dynamics that support them in reclaiming the parts of themselves that were lost or damaged because of the abuse.

The remainder of this book will present information gleaned from both written resources and the interviews with contributors. The treatment model that is presented outlines a therapeutic healing process for male victims of sexual abuse. This chapter discusses the general principles of this treatment model, describes the general stages of healing, and identifies issues that can hinder the therapeutic process.

THERAPEUTIC MODEL FOR
MALE VICTIMS OF SEXUAL ABUSE

Describing a general process of recovery or healing is a difficult task. Every recovered abuse victim has his own story to tell of this journey. However, in order to work effectively with abuse survivors, each therapist must develop a generic "map of recovery" that he or she will use to guide the therapeutic process. Although this "map" will no doubt be conceptualized in different ways at different stages of the therapist's career, each therapist needs, at any given time, to be able to articulate the changes that the interventions used are designed to facilitate in his or her clients.

The model described in this text suggests that healing from sexual trauma is a process that leads the survivor from a position of making abuse-reactive life decisions, based on past learning, to a new position of making proactive life decisions and choices based on present needs. As the survivor makes his unconscious coping strategies conscious, his personal autonomy increases. Flashbacks of the abuse become reclaimed memories, inexplicable fears and anxieties become associations to present environmental triggers that echo abuse-related experiences, and some chronic somatic complaints become the signals for recognizing unmet physical or emotional needs.

As the survivor decodes his behaviors, thoughts, and feelings, he begins to recognize how his belief system was shaped by his victimization and by his reactions to this experience. This recognition opens the door for him to develop new life choices and options. The experience of learning, practicing, and integrating new attitudes and behavior is a spiraling process, not a linear one. Often, old patterns have to be revisited many times before they are replaced with new ones. However, "With each new cycle, [the survivor's]...capacity to feel, to remember, to make lasting changes, is strengthened" (Bass & Davis, 1988, p. 59).

The effects of sexual abuse are complicated by other forms of neglect and abuse that were present in the victim's childhood and compounded by the damage resulting from the development of initially adaptive but ultimately self-destructive coping behaviors. Trauma of a *sexual* nature shames and degrades the victim at the level of his existential core. Given the complexities of long-term trauma, "...the process of resolution for child sexual abuse is of a long-term rather than a short-term nature" (Courtois, 1991, p. 51).

Survivors of abuse can never change the facts of the abuse. They cannot eradicate the abuse from their personal histories. However, they can change their relationship to this history and they can change the effects these events have on their lives.

For personal change to be authentic and integrated into a survivor's life, ample time to test and explore new alternative behaviors must be present. Contributors generally worked with their survivor clients for a minimum of a year and often for much longer, in order to bring about lasting and substantive change.

Not all of a survivor's problems are related to his experience of childhood sexual abuse. Other life traumas play their part. Therapists must be discerning in their diagnostic skills; they must take care not to simplistically attribute their clients' issues solely to their sexual trauma if this is not an accurate assignation.

Therapy for sexual abuse survivors has many facets. Reducing a survivor's sense of isolation, facilitating his emotional discharge, challenging his cognitive distortions, normalizing his experience, and educating him about abuse processes are all part of the journey (Briere, 1989). Nurturing his spirituality (using this word in its most general sense) and rekindling his hope are also important. By the end of the journey, the survivor is aware that "...he is an adult who can care for himself in a better way than he was cared for as a child" (Dimock, 1988, p. 217).

BASIC PRINCIPLES OF MALE SURVIVOR TREATMENT

The contributors to this study are experienced therapists who have a broad range of both experience and theory to call upon in their work with male survivors. They utilize a wide range of theoretical orientations, including family systems models, feminist therapy models, cognitive-behavioral restructuring processes, hypnosis, and psychodynamic approaches.

All of the contributors are eclectic in their theoretical approach to working with male survivors. Although some favor one particular theoretical model over others, none of the contributors uses one theory base exclusively. They agree that using a theoretical model that is suitable to the client and his presenting issues is more important than being loyal to a theory irrespective of the client's issues. If, for example, a client is very cognitive in his presentation, they suggest initially using a theoretical orientation, such as cognitive restructuring, that will join with the client's process. More affectively focused methods of therapy, such as gestalt therapy or psychodrama, are not used until such time as the client can experience his affect with some comfort.

Despite the wide range in the contributor's theoretical orientations, they agree that the following key concepts underlie successful therapy with male survivors.

Empowerment

All the contributors agree that assisting their clients to regain their personal power is an essential component of successful sexual abuse treatment. Acknowledging a client's strengths and validating the survival skills he has developed, however functional or dysfunctional they may be in his present life context, is crucial. A survivor's very presence in a therapist's office is living proof that he had what it took to survive the impact of sexual abuse. However great his need to transform his survival skills into more adaptive processes, he needs to recognize that his present level of skill has ensured his survival thus far.

Client-Focused, Client-Paced Therapy

The therapist and client must work in partnership while addressing the client's abuse-related concerns. If a therapist acts as an authority figure in the therapeutic relationship, he or she invites the transference that was initially formed in the abuse experience when the offender had power over the victim. Although such transference may eventually be constructively resolved, it threatens the formulation of the therapeutic relationship in the short run. It imposes stresses on both client and therapist that are generally unduly taxing and counterproductive.

This does not mean to say that clinicians do not bring skills and aware-ness that can help their clients' recovery. They do. However, the frame in which the therapeutic process occurs is one in which the therapist can act as a "consultant" to his client and the client is an informed "con-sumer" who determines the services he wishes to "purchase."

> ...the client is the authority with regard to what postabuse trauma
> feels like, what seems to help and whether therapy is progressing as
> it should.... (Briere, 1989, p. 59)

Not only is the survivor the expert on his abuse-related experience, he is also responsible for his own healing process. A therapist can facilitate a client's recovery, but cannot take responsibility for it. Both the client and the therapist need to be very clear about who is responsible for mak-ing changes in the client's life. If this is not clear, the client can remain in a victim position in which he doesn't claim responsibility for his life and the therapist runs the risk of becoming either a rescuer or a persecutor as he or she tries to motivate the client to change.

Linking the Past to the Present

Many survivors are not aware of a connection between their experi-ence of being sexually abused as a child and the problematic issues they face in their adult lives. Because they have either repressed their abuse memories or disowned their abuse experience and claim that it has had no impact on them, they don't have a context for understanding their current behavior. Often, this leaves them feeling crazy or ashamed. When symp-toms are seen as "a creative adaptation to highly negative circumstances rather than an expression of psychopathology" (Courtois, 1991, p. 50), survivors are able to start their journey of healing and recovery.

As survivors reclaim their memories and discharge their repressed af-fect, they can begin to understand and change dysfunctional patterns in their lives. When they develop an understanding that all their behavior makes sense, they begin to decode their experience rather than disowning or judging it. For some survivors, so-called "psychotic" episodes are PTSD flashbacks or expressions of MPD. Seeing himself as an abuse survivor who is exhibiting common abuse-related symptoms, rather than as a mental patient whose only hope is medication, can support a client in making positive change. This does not mean that some survivors will not require psychotropic drugs or hospitalization. However, in general, the sense of normalcy that survivors regain when their present behavior is connected to past events supports the healing process.

Growth and Learning Model

The contributors agree that survivors need to be invited into the therapeutic process with the understanding that "We all do the best we can at all times." Skill deficits, overwhelming emotions, or confused internal states result in inappropriate or dysfunctional responses to events in a survivor's present life. Changing these maladaptive responses depends on learning and integrating new skills, increasing awareness and understanding of internal processes, and acknowledging emotional states.

Replacing maladaptive patterns and beliefs with functional ones and assimilating these changes in a supportive environment are essential ingredients of the recovery process. Most of the challenges that clients face in their lives do not occur in therapy sessions. Clients need support to transfer the learning that occurs during the therapeutic process into their daily lives. Therapists need to assist clients to develop structures that allow them to anchor their psychosocial growth so that it becomes habitual behavior.

Integration

Healing from sexual abuse is, in part, a process of reclaiming lost or "stuck" parts of the self. Survivors need to be told: "Bad things happened to you. You were not bad." Often, at the time of the abuse, given his cognitive, affective, and physical immaturity, the victim decided that he was being abused because he deserved to be abused. He concluded that he himself was responsible for being abused. He believed that shameful or dangerous parts of himself had caused his victimization. He then, unconsciously, repressed or dissociated those shameful or dangerous parts in a misguided attempt to make himself normal. These undervalued parts of self were put out of conscious awareness, only to intrude later in unconscious form.

Most survivors need to reclaim and integrate devalued parts of themselves. Men who deny or repress their victimization experience, yet display abuse-related symptoms such as drug or alcohol abuse, need to become aware that they have complex and sometimes conflicting internal needs. They need to recognize that as well as having an adult persona, they also incorporate a damaged internal child who may continue to act problematically regardless of the survivor's chronological age. When the various parts of the self are in communication with one another and no part is devalued or ignored, the survivor will experience greater health and balance.

Recognition of Grief

Survivors need to acknowledge the losses that occurred in their lives as a result of childhood sexual abuse. They lost their childhood innocence when the abuse began. Their inherent sexual clock was prematurely started. Often close family relationships are lost to them. Many must cope with the aftermath of abuse without family support. Part of the recovery process for survivors is to grieve their losses. The stages of denial, bargaining, anger, sadness, and acceptance form part of a survivor's healing journey (Hunter, 1990a).

Safety

The earliest stage of psychosocial development in Erikson's theory of development is basic trust. This stage underlies all others and forms the bedrock for further psychosocial growth. By definition, a survivor's trust in others has been breached. Either by seductive or aggressive means, he has been violated by another human being. When a survivor enters therapy, he brings his lack of trust in others with him.

At the beginning of the therapeutic process, trust in the therapist has to be earned. The therapist will have to address the client's lack of trust by ensuring that the therapeutic process is safe. This means that clients will not be expected to trust either the therapist or the therapeutic process until such time as this happens naturally. However, each client will be expected to identify his needs regarding safety in the therapeutic process. The therapist helps the client by gently but persistently *soliciting* these needs. In addition, clearly discussing the therapeutic ground rules and the therapeutic contract increases safety in the therapeutic process. (These issues will be presented in detail in Chapter 4.)

Recognition That Abuse Is Both Personal and Cultural

Although sexual abuse is a personal experience, it is intrinsically linked to larger cultural forces. An analysis of the cultural and political forces that create sexual abuse is not generally part of therapy. However, it is impossible to address a client's postabuse responses without acknowledging that both client and therapist are members of a culture that permits sexual violence and exploitation.

The necessity of addressing cultural and social issues is even stronger when victimization due to sexual abuse is compounded by other kinds of victimization such as racial discrimination, homophobic prejudice, or poverty. In such cases, the victim's issues are likely to be a complex outcome of concurrent victimization processes and they must be therapeutically addressed as such.

One part of therapy with male survivors involves debunking various social myths regarding sexual abuse. Many such myths relate to a survivor's sense of his masculinity or questions about his sexual orientation; the necessary "debunking" cannot occur without examining cultural values and social expectations. Learning how social forces have been internalized and incorporated into the survivor's sense of self thus becomes a part of successful therapy. Often, as either a direct or indirect outgrowth of therapy, survivors reexamine social and cultural values. As a result, they gain greater freedom to fully accept the realities of their own lives, including their victimization.

Transference and Countertransference

Male survivors of sexual abuse, like other therapy clients, tend to interpret and shape their therapeutic experience in ways that conform to their worldview. If a client believes that all men are sexually inappropriate or that no one will ever be able to help him, he will bring these beliefs into the therapeutic process. He will unconsciously attempt to replicate his childhood beliefs with the therapist.

Therapists need to be aware of transference and countertransference dynamics in order to intervene skillfully. Therapists often have unresolved or partially resolved personal issues that coincide with their clients' dynamics. Under these circumstances, it is easy for a therapist to take a client's issues or "transference bait" personally. This is not helpful. Instead the therapist must work with the client to see how his patterns of understanding the world and interacting with others were established. It cannot be emphasized strongly enough how essential good supervision is in helping therapists navigate transference/countertransference dynamics successfully.

Contributors also noted some therapeutic stances that are counterproductive when one is working with male survivors.

Survivors don't need their therapists to be models of perfection. As a consequence of their painful childhoods, survivors have often constructed fantasies of "perfect relationships" in which they imagine themselves finally having all their unmet needs recognized and addressed. These images of perfection are as dysfunctional a map for real relationships as the abusive relationships they experienced in childhood. Being authentic is an important quality that therapists can model for clients.

Therapists need to respect their own human limitations—"...therapists are human beings who inevitably make mistakes and who may not always be able to maintain the empathic bond that guides accurate helping behaviors" (Briere, 1989, p. 59). When therapists honestly own their mistakes and take the new information gained from making these mistakes into account in their subsequent work with clients, they model a process of trial-and-error learning that helps clients acknowledge their own human limits.

Therapists who have been trained to respond to clients like a "blank screen" need to adjust this style when working with male survivors. A neutral stance can be perceived by a client as a lack of responsiveness to his pain or as a judgement about his experience; it may leave him feeling confused, frightened, and isolated. Survivors require a responsive, psychoeducational therapeutic alliance that validates their experience and helps them to move beyond its negative effects. Therapists who work with male survivors need to be overtly empathic, accepting, and supportive.

STAGES OF THERAPY—A FOUR-PHASE MODEL

From the therapist's perspective, therapy with male survivors has four distinct phases. This four-phase model of therapy is helpful both as an analogous description of the recovery process for male survivors and as an analytical tool to assist in case management and treatment planning.

The four phases are:

    1 — Breaking Silence
    2 — The Victim Stage
    3 — The Survivor Phase
    4 — The Thriver Stage

(N.B. In following chapters, interventions are organized in relation to this four-phase model and they are presented according to the therapeutic phase in which they are most appropriately used.)

Individual clients will spend more or less time in any given phase of healing and some phases will overlap with one another. Some clients will stay in one phase for a long time, reaching a plateau in their growth; it may be advisable to take a planned break from therapy during these times. However, in general, each phase is associated with distinct issues and demands different skills from the therapist.

At all times, the therapeutic process for male survivors needs to be relevant to individual needs. Identifying a client's phase of healing can help a therapist to skillfully and strategically focus the therapy to meet this client's unique requirements.

Before beginning abuse-focused therapy, clients need information about the therapeutic process. Knowing ahead of time that recovery tends to be long-term rather than short-term and that the healing journey is not a linear one helps clients to make decisions about their investment in treatment. (The client engagement process is discussed in Chapter 9.) Each client will have to decide how to allocate his resources (e.g., time, money, etc.) to support his recovery. Relatively accurate and candid predictions about the therapeutic process, including the length of the journey, will help clients make these decisions.

Giving clients a cognitive map with which to understand the healing process can be a supportive intervention. Although the concept of a four-phase model of healing is somewhat abstract, being able to identify which phase he is currently in helps a client know where he is headed and what kind of process he can anticipate en route. Whether or not clients want such a map, it is essential that each therapist uses one to guide his interventions. The different phases of the four-phase model are described below:

Phase 1—Breaking Silence

Acknowledging to himself that he was sexually abused as a child is the first step a survivor must take to heal from this experience. Reaching out to others for support and validation of this experience, as well as breaking the silence that has surrounded the secret of the abuse, is an important step.

Survivors come in different ways to the realization that they were abused. For some men, their memories surface during therapy for issues that are not abuse-related, when they begin to realize that their patterns of behavior are the result of childhood sexual trauma. Other men have never forgotten being abused, but have discounted the impact of these events on their lives or have never labelled them as abuse. Yet others have a sudden realization while watching a TV show about sexual abuse, or while reading a book that refers to sexual abuse, that they have themselves been victimized.

However it happens, acknowledging his sexual victimization is the beginning of a survivor's healing process. Some men will seek support and help to cope with this realization by immediately going to see a counsellor or by attending a self-help group. Many others wait a long time before they share this information with others.

When a therapist is treating a man for other issues, but suspects a history of abuse because of the symptoms his client is experiencing, he is ethically bound to explore the possibility of childhood trauma with his client. Even if the client denies a history of abuse, the clinician must raise the possibility of childhood trauma and its associated symptoms (Courtois, 1991). Clearly, if the client has no associations with having been sexually abused, the therapist should not insist on following this line of inquiry. But as long as the symptoms suggest childhood trauma, the clinician must continue to leave the possibility open. Bringing the client to awareness and acknowledgement of childhood trauma may take some time and requires rapport and trust in the therapist/client relationship. The client may also need to develop life skills (e.g., communication, assertiveness, anxiety management, etc.) before he has sufficient ego strength to manage his emotional responses to acknowledging his sexual abuse.

Some therapists are reluctant to pursue questions about abuse if their client has no memory of having been abused. "False Memory Syndrome," in which therapists are thought to create their clients' memories of abuse by planting hypnotic suggestions, is currently a topic of much debate in therapeutic circles. I believe that concerns about creating false memories are secondary to giving a client feedback that his symptoms suggest a history of childhood trauma, which may include sexual abuse. Until such time as this possibility can be clearly eliminated, it bears examination.

Phase 2—The Victim Stage

The main focus of this phase of therapy is to validate the client's abuse history, to build a safe therapeutic process with the client, and to provide educational information about the effects of sexual abuse on its victims. Unless a client has intense flashbacks or other affectively demanding concerns, much of the work in this phase will be cognitively focused.

Men often need support in acknowledging their victimization. Even if they can recall the sexually intrusive events that have happened to them, many men don't call them "abusive." Educating clients about power differences, coercion, misrepresenting adult reality, the use of threats and lies to gain compliance, and so on can assist male victims to fully claim their experience.

The therapist needs to find a balance between staying focused on abuse-related material and not pushing a client beyond his own comfort zone. If the process becomes too intense or if the client perceives the therapist as trying to control the therapy process, it is quite likely that the client will shut down in the face of this replication of an abusive dynamic.

To the extent that the client's memories permit, he will be asked to develop a "sexual abuse autobiography" during this phase of therapy. Remembering how he was groomed for the abuse, who offended against him, how often the abuse occurred, what explicitly happened, what his reactions were at the time, whether or not he told anyone and what, if anything, he liked about the experience are areas to investigate at this stage. Talking openly about the abuse and continuing to challenge any denial of the experience are primary tasks for this therapeutic phase.

Clients who have defended against their abuse memories by developing substance or process addictions find themselves in somewhat of a "Catch-22" situation. If they maintain their addiction, they are unable to process their abuse history effectively; if they give up their addiction, they are often flooded by uncontrollable memories and feelings, which may lead to a relapse. Therapists have to carefully monitor addictive behavior at this phase of therapy.

If a client is not yet ready to surrender an addiction, he can be supported by the recommendation that he develop other means of addressing his anxiety before he begins to process his abuse history. Occasional relapses are predictable for addicted clients, but when the addiction is still used as a primary coping strategy, abuse-related therapy will be counter-productive and it is generally contraindicated.

The therapist needs to teach stress management and self-care skills during this phase, so that as the therapeutic focus becomes more affective, clients have functional ways of attending to their emotions. Ensuring that clients have active support systems in place or focusing on building these supports are therapeutic tasks in the Victim Phase.

In this phase, clients will generally feel some emotional relief at realizing that the problems they face in their lives are not the result of being crazy, but the outcome of being sexually abused as a child. As they gain information about dissociative processes and other coping strategies, they begin to feel more normal and hopeful about the future.

The transition between the Victim and Survivor Phases of therapy is marked by the client's ability to place full responsibility for the abuse on the offender. When the client recognizes that he was a victim in an abusive relationship and that the abuse was a reflection not of his worth as a person, but of his offender's unresolved problems, he moves into the next phase of therapy.

Phase 3—The Survivor Phase

The Survivor Phase of therapy describes the often arduous work of repairing clients' emotional, cognitive, and behaviorial dysfunctions. This is a push/pull stage of therapy. The client's maladaptive life patterns are slowly replaced by functional sequences as the client takes the risk of developing new coping strategies. Walking a fine line between containment and expression, as well as finding a workable balance of both, is the key to success during this phase of therapy.

Often, clients become discouraged in this phase. Because they are reclaiming their previously blocked affective processes, they are more aware of feelings of fear, pain, rage, or sadness. They feel unstable as they discard old methods of coping and substitute new ones that are still relatively untested and awkward to use. They feel as if therapy has made them worse rather than better. Many cases of premature termination occur in this phase as clients lose their faith in ever being able to make significant changes.

At this point in therapy, clinicians must be steady and focused. They need to remind their clients that discouragement is to be expected in the Survivor Phase. The original momentum of addressing the abuse has worn off and some weariness has set in. The therapist must nonetheless continue to help the client identify his feelings and challenge his thinking errors and distorted beliefs. Throughout this phase, the therapist must affirm the client's strength and courage. By validating the painfulness and difficulty of this stage of the therapeutic work and by acknowledging the positive changes made to date, the therapist maps out the therapeutic journey, thus supporting the client's recovery. The Survivor Phase of therapy is identified by particular therapeutic tasks. Affective responses are identified and worked with during this stage. Becoming acquainted with a wide range of emotions and exploring ways in which these feeling states can be expressed can be a slow and fear-filled process. However, as survivors become more familiar with their previously dissociated feelings, they begin to experience a greater sense of wholeness and well-being. Habitual dysfunctional cognitive and behavioral patterns are also worked with during this therapeutic stage. Thinking errors and self-defeating behavioral sequences are identified and replaced by healthier substitutes. New self-care skills are learned and practiced.

During the Survivor Phase, new skills need to be practised outside of therapy sessions. Throughout this therapeutic stage sessions may involve both spontaneous and planned abreactive processes. (Working with abreactions will be discussed in Chapter 6.) At times, clients may need to take a planned break from therapy and integrate their learning before continuing the process.

The transition between the Survivor Phase and the Thriver Phase is marked by the client's readiness to take back his own power; this will frequently be manifested by the client's readiness to confront his offender, either in reality or, more often, symbolically. This is not a reactive stand taken in defiance against the offender; instead, it represents an integrated change in which the client no longer feels that the offender has power over his life.

Phase 4—The Thriver Phase

When the client reaches the Thriver Phase, he begins to feel hopeful once again. From an empowered perspective of having changed previously dysfunctional coping patterns he can articulate the ways in which he was affected by having been abused. He realizes that the outcome of successful therapy is not "living happily ever after," but having the skills and resources that he needs to address the difficulties that occur in his life.

Thrivers feel responsible for their lives and they believe that they have many options to choose from in addressing their life problems, both past and present. The abuse is no longer seen as a central issue in the client's self-identification; his image of himself has shifted into the present and he trusts his adult self.

During the Thriver Phase, client and therapist must begin the process of termination. Termination needs to be managed so that the client can leave the therapeutic process at his own pace. In addition, clients should be given plenty of permission to return to therapy should they experience a resurgence of symptoms or should new abuse memories surface.

The therapist must be very careful not to compromise therapist/client boundaries by permitting double relationships to develop. Clients need their therapists to remain available to them for potential future consultation; any double relationship, such as when a therapist becomes a friend, lover, landlord, or business partner to a client, jeopardizes the safety of the therapeutic relationship. Risk of such double relationships might arise when the therapist is himself a survivor with needs for social support from relatively "recovered" fellow survivors or when a recovering client is seen as a professional ally who can assist in furthering desperately needed services for survivors.

Chapter 4

General Therapeutic Considerations

This chapter describes processes common to all modalities of abuse-focused therapy. Therapeutic contracts, assessment procedures, and evaluation processes are discussed in some detail. In addition, behaviors and circumstances that contraindicate abuse-focused therapy are outlined.

All the primary psychotherapeutic modalities—individual, group, couple and family therapy—can be used to treat the effects of childhood sexual abuse. For adult male survivors, individual and group treatment are generally considered the most effective treatment formats.

Although therapists always need to be flexible and to accommodate to the individual needs of clients, the contributors agree that male survivors are generally best served by first engaging in individual therapy and then moving into group therapy with concurrent individual work on an as-needed basis. Couple or family work may be used as a regular adjunct to the therapeutic process, if this supports a client's recovery. Body work may be a useful addition to a client's healing primarily during the Thriver Phase of therapy.

Contributors were quick to point out that the ideal and the possible are not always identical regarding the provision of service to male survivors. Circumstances often dictate the realities that both clients and therapists face. Many clients' choices about therapeutic resources are determined by financial considerations rather than by need. Some geographic areas have limited clinical resources and individual treatment is the only type of therapy available. In other areas, group treatment is available, but there aren't enough individual therapists.

Certain aspects of therapy are common to all therapeutic modalities. Developing a therapeutic contract, identifying issues that are contraindicators for therapy, conducting a thorough assessment, and evaluating therapeutic outcomes are essential ingredients of therapy, regardless of the treatment modality. These generic components of treatment are discussed below.

DEVELOPING A THERAPEUTIC CONTRACT

Both sexual abuse and therapy are interpersonal processes. Because of this similarity, for therapy to be healing and not harming, it must occur in a context of ethical and clinical integrity. Both clients and therapists need to have clear guidelines about the relational aspects of therapy. A therapeutic contract clarifies the *roles* and *rules* of the therapeutic process. Because therapy is not a static process, the contract has to be renegotiated as therapy progresses. For many survivors, developing a therapeutic contract is an opportunity to practice negotiating their needs.

Therapeutic contracts may be written or verbal, depending on the therapist's and client's respective personal styles. Often the formal aspects of the agreement (fee schedules, session times, etc.) will be written down, while the informal, spontaneous aspects of the therapeutic process (planning how to work with particular issues) will be negotiated verbally. For clients who are highly dissociative, writing down therapeutic agreements can be helpful; a written contract provides a tangible record to refer to if they cannot recall what happened during a session.

Some therapists use the contracting process to give their clients information about how they work. For instance, some therapists explicitly inform their clients that they will not become sexually or socially involved with them or create dual roles with them. They tell clients that it is the client's right to pace the therapeutic process and determine its duration. They explicitly give clients permission to debrief or question any interactions that are hurtful, puzzling, or unclear, so that the client always has an opportunity to examine the therapeutic process. They may briefly explain their therapeutic style, so that clients can be informed consumers when selecting a therapist.

Spending time developing a therapeutic contract is reassuring to new clients. A clear contract circumvents later problems since guidelines for behaviors and actions are outlined prior to needing to use them. Key elements that should be discussed when developing a therapeutic contract are outlined below.

Information Boundaries

Clients need to be assured that the therapeutic process is confidential and that their personal history will be respected by the therapist. However, they also need to know that if they abuse themselves or others (including the therapist) or are violent towards their surroundings, it will be considered grounds for breaking therapeutic confidentiality. Therapists should be knowledgeable about the legal aspects of reporting abuse. They must share this information with their clients when applicable. Clients must be informed that if they disclose information about present abuse situations or abusers who have access to young children, police and child welfare agencies must be informed. Safety concerns always precede concerns about confidentiality.

Because the abuse occurred in secrecy, some clients are anxious about therapeutic confidentiality. They may need to examine the boundary of confidentiality in some detail in order to feel reassured that therapy will not replicate the abuse process. Clients who are afraid that they will not be able to control the therapeutic process are often reassured when a therapist asks questions such as, "How will you, let me know if your therapy is going in a direction that is not helpful to you?"

Fees

Clients need clear information about how much a therapist charges for his or her services and how he or she expects to be paid. Therapists must be clear about how flexible they are willing to be about fee collection. Clear fee policies assist both clients and therapists.

Structure of Sessions

Clients need information about the duration and frequency of sessions. Although these may at times need to be renegotiated to meet unique circumstances, having clear time boundaries is an important way to differentiate therapy from abuse.

Touch Boundaries

It is imperative for clients to control when and how they are touched during therapy. Each client must always determine his own touch boundary. During the abuse, the victim was not in charge of how he was touched; therapists must take care not to replicate this experience during therapy sessions. Even routine social rituals, such as shaking hands, should occur only if initiated by the client.

Similarly, each therapist must ensure that his or her own comfort zones regarding touch are not infringed; if a client requests a hug, but the therapist is not comfortable with this contact, the therapist needs to own and honor his or her personal boundary. Such behavior presents the client with a positive role model for respectful touch boundaries.

Crisis and Emergency Plans

Prior to engaging in therapy, clients need information about the kind of support they will receive from their therapist outside of scheduled sessions. Clients need to know their therapist's boundaries regarding telephone access and whether the therapist is available for unscheduled emergency sessions. When a therapist goes on holiday, clients need to know whether their therapist has arranged for coverage by another therapist should an emergency arise.

Planning for possible crises can reduce a client's level of anxiety. Should a client become sufficiently self-harming that hospitalization is required for his personal safety, he will respond to this plan more easily if he has previously agreed to its merits. Developing emergency contingency plans with clients before engaging in therapy is a useful early step.

Some clinicians have a prepared handout for their clients that outlines their policies and procedures. This can reduce the amount of session time that is spent on this information and it leaves the client with a concrete resource for future reference.

CONTRAINDICATORS FOR ABUSE-RELATED THERAPY

In order for abuse-related therapy to be healing rather than retraumatizing, clients need to be ready to address their sexual victimization and therapists need to have sufficient skill to ensure that the therapy is emotionally corrective. Timeliness is an important variable to consider when offering this kind of therapy. These are some of the main reasons that abuse-related therapy would be contraindicated.

Ongoing Life Crises

If a survivor's life is currently crisis-ridden, working intensively on past trauma will generally only exacerbate his current instability. Clients who have difficulty keeping a job or earning enough money to meet basic needs, or who are in the midst of a relationship breakdown, are not good candidates for abuse-related therapy. They need to focus on these more immediate issues before they engage in abuse-related work.

Clients who are actively violent or in an abusive relationship need to address these patterns before they are ready to look beyond these symptoms at the deeper causes of their behaviors. Suicidal or psychotic survivors need to manage these mental health issues before focusing on their victimization.

Clients who have active substance or process addictions are not good candidates for abuse-focused therapy until they have developed healthier emotional coping strategies. Although some therapists will work with clients after only six months of sobriety or drug-free time, most therapists working with ex-addicts follow the rule-of-thumb of "one year clean and sober."

Lack of Social Support

If a survivor is very isolated, therapy must focus on developing social skills and building community before moving into abuse-related processes. Neither a therapist nor a client will be well served if the therapist is the only source of support in the client's life. A lack of social support reinforces clients' dysfunctional beliefs; it supports their self-image of not being deserving of caring and their belief that their victimization experiences are too shameful to be shared with others.

Therapy is only a small part of a client's life. Clients need to have companionship and caring within their natural communities as well as in their therapy. Many clients attend 12-step programs as a means of developing new avenues of social support. Interaction with others, in both therapeutic and social ways, is an important part of the recovery process.

Lack of Motivation to Change

Some clients come to therapy because other people think it would help them. If a client doesn't recognize that he has a problem or that certain aspects of his life are unsatisfactory, he has no motivation to change. Therapy that is focused on childhood sexual abuse requires a commitment on the part of the client; he will have to address painful issues of betrayal and loss in the course of his recovery. If a client does not have an investment in making changes and achieving therapeutic goals during the course of therapy, he is not a good candidate for abuse-related work.

Therapist's Limitations

If a therapist is not available to work with a client on an ongoing basis or does not feel competent to work with abuse-focused issues, he or she should refer the client elsewhere. It is very traumatic for a survivor who is beginning to explore the possibility of trusting another person, namely his therapist, to suddenly have this process threatened because the therapist changes jobs or has to terminate the therapy for some other reason. Of course, unanticipated events will occur in both therapists' and clients' lives; however, whenever possible, therapists must respect their clients' needs for stability and safety and try to avoid premature termination.

Breaking the Therapeutic Contract

If a client is unwilling to follow the negotiated terms of the therapeutic contract, he is not a suitable candidate for abuse-related work. Clients who will not accept responsibility for their own behavior; who threaten the safety of others, including the therapist; or who consistently break agreements about session times or fee payment need to address these issues before they open the doors to their victimization experiences. The emotions that emerge during the recovery process tend to be intense; if a client is not willing to be accountable in his relationships with himself and others, abuse-focused therapy can be dangerous.

CLIENT ASSESSMENT

When a clinician is conducting an assessment with an abuse survivor or someone who may be an abuse survivor, it is very important that he or she actively solicit information about the abuse and its impact on the client. If you wait for the client to raise these issues, they may never surface. A client may interpret a therapist's lack of active questioning about abuse as support for his own minimization or denial. A client's shame about having been abused maintains his silence about this event; the therapist must gently but actively support and encourage the client to break silence and challenge his feelings of shame.

Therapists must be careful not to make assumptions about their clients' abuse experiences; clients must be given time and space to tell their own story in their own words. You can generally assume that most clients will disclose their abuse histories in chunks; clients test their therapists' reactions to partial disclosures before they feel safe enough to make a full and complete disclosure. Usually, the parts of the abuse experience that a client feels the greatest shame about will be the last to be told. Therapists have to walk a fine line between opening the door for information about the abuse to surface and being too intrusive.

Therapists' assessment questions need to be specific and worded in a nonjudgmental way so as to elicit useful diagnostic material. For example, instead of asking, "Do you have a sleeping disorder?" ask the more open-ended and less threatening question, "What is your regular sleeping pattern?" For many clients, dysfunctional coping strategies are ego-syntonic or culturally sanctioned and they do not appear abnormal. Clinicians must ensure that the questions they ask are precise, straightforward, and nonthreatening.

Some clients' histories are shocking and very upsetting, so clinicians must be prepared to hear the answers to the questions they ask. For example, questions about sexual habits and practices that would be embarrassing in a social context need to be asked as part of a thorough assessment. It is essential that the therapist be comfortable asking questions about masturbation, sexual fantasies, sexual practices, anger, fear, and other culturally sensitive or emotionally loaded issues. If the therapist is uncomfortable, this will be communicated to the client, who may then disclose only partial information in an attempt to make the therapist feel more at ease.

In general, the more thorough the assessment, the fewer the surprises that will emerge in therapy. If during the assessment process it becomes apparent that a client is highly dissociative, then the clinician can prepare to work with someone who has possible MPD or other related symptoms. Client confidence and safety are increased by predictability, so time spent in conducting a thorough assessment is generally repaid later in the therapeutic process. Some clients exhibit symptoms associated with abuse, but they do not have a cognitive memory of having been victimized. In such cases, broad, open-ended questions such as "I'm wondering if you experienced some trauma in your past; the things that you're telling me about yourself seem to indicate that you had to learn to handle some very traumatic situations" can support the client. It is important that clients who have repressed memories do not feel ashamed because they are unable to recollect their experiences. They must not be forced to remember events before their unconscious is ready to do so. Therapists must let the abuse history come from the client and not contaminate the therapeutic process by placing expectations on the client to disclose memories prematurely. When a client recovers repressed memories in a timely fashion, he trusts his own recollection and doesn't undermine his recovery by questioning the validity of his experience.

If a clinician is uncertain about the dynamics that a client is presenting, he or she should consult with a knowledgeable colleague. The assessment process lays the foundation for the rest of the therapy; it is important that clients not be over- or underpathologized as a result of this process.

Certain key areas need to be carefully assessed. These are discussed below.

General Family/Social History

Frequently, victims of sexual abuse have other traumatic events in addition to having been sexually abused that have shaped their lives. Clinicians need to conduct a thorough family and social history to understand the important events (and people) in a client's life. Problematic areas, such as violence or a lack of social support, need to be assessed. However, clients also need a clear inventory of their strengths and resources. Successful patterns and helpful strengths are as important as problem areas and trauma.

The survivor's current life patterns must be carefully assessed. The client's status vis-à-vis work, relationships, health, parenting roles and skills, and so on need to be determined. Until a client's day-to-day life is functioning adequately, focusing on abuse-related events can be countertherapeutic.

Sexual History

During the assessment, a survivor may or may not be able to disclose specific information about his sexual victimization. If the therapist frames his questions carefully, he can increase his client's comfort in sharing whatever conscious memories he does have. Asking the client to "Tell me as much about your childhood sexual experiences as you think I need to know in order to understand what happened to you" can sometimes elicit more information than a very direct question because the client is less anxious when responding to the request.

Dimock (1988) encourages clients to write down their sexual histories. This gives the client more privacy and greater safety and control. Information is then shared with the therapist as the client chooses, leaving the client in charge of his disclosure process. Since many clients are afraid that the therapist will take a voyeuristic interest in their sexual past (as the abuser did), reducing the level of threat and shame in presenting their sexual histories is very important. Dimock suggests providing clients with a means of categorizing their abuse experiences. He gives his clients a list of four categories of sexual behaviour with several examples in each. These are:

(a) chargeable offenses (anal and oral sex, fondling, intercourse, and so on);

(b) growing up in a sexualized atmosphere (excessive interest on the part of family members in peeping or exposing, open presence of pornography, covert sexualized touch, and the like);

(c) intrusive behaviours (sexual punishments, unusual interest in and questions about sexuality, unnecessary enemas, supervised baths beyond a reasonable age, and applications of medication to the genital area when the child is able to do this alone, etc.); and

(d) inappropriate relationships where the child is placed in an adult role with sexual implications (regular sleeping with a parent, date-like relationships, confiding in the child especially about sexual information, etc.).

To the extent that is possible, the survivor's sexual history should include information about specific behaviors that occurred during the abuse, who was present, how old the client was when the abuse was occurring, how old his abuser(s) was, how he felt at the time, and whether he has sensory memories (taste, smell, etc.) from the abuse (Dimock, 1988). If the client has made previous disclosures, he should be asked about these experiences. Whether he was believed or not and whether he was supported or not can have an impact on his expectation about how you will receive his present disclosure of victimization.

Coping Strategies

Clients need to be asked about the ways, both functional and dysfunctional, that they have coped with the impacts of having been sexually abused. Many clients are unable to articulate their coping mechanisms; however, it is often the dysfunctional coping strategies the client has been using that have brought him into therapy.

Dissociative behaviors need to be assessed. Frequently, educating clients about dissociative processes and increasing their awareness of when they are engaging in these behaviors is a necessary step before a full assessment. (See Appendix C for a copy of the Dissociative Experiences Scale [DES] which can be used to assess dissociative tendencies.)

Survivors often exhibit dominant sympathetic nervous system symptoms such as an exaggerated startle response or chronic muscle tension. Many survivors live in a chronic state of emotional fear and anxiety. Hence, the normal balance between their sympathetic and parasympathetic nervous systems is disturbed. Anxiety attacks, excessive irritability, and hypervigilance are common symptoms experienced by sexual trauma survivors. Eating and sleeping patterns are often disrupted. Difficulty in falling asleep or a pattern of waking up in the middle of the night, an inability to digest food, or rapid weight loss indicates an overworked sympathetic nervous system.

Many survivors develop addictions or compulsive behaviors in an effort to mask their abuse-related emotions. The very issues that the addictions were developed to cover will resurface during therapy. As Dimock (1988) states, while occasional flight into compulsive behaviors is expected during therapy, continuous involvement in these activities makes it very difficult for therapy to continue.

Abuse-Reactive Perpetration

As discussed in Chapter 2, some victims, either because of identification with the aggressor or unconscious efforts to understand their own victimization, will have sexually perpetrated against others. This activity needs to be assessed in the early part of treatment. If a survivor is currently sexually offending or has done so in the past, he must be held accountable for his actions. In most jurisdictions, the therapist is legally bound to report any offenses his client discloses. Even if the offending was a very infrequent event during the client's adolescence, the client needs to acknowledge this component of his behavior and address it in therapy.

Asking questions about abuse-reactive perpetration can be difficult. Many victims have not reenacted their victimization and will be upset by any insinuation that they might have done so. Phrasing the question in a skillful manner (such as in the following example) can be helpful: "Often, victims of abuse find that they want to do what happened to them to someone else. Did this ever happen to you?"

Treatment Motivation/Goals

Therapists need to assess their clients' goals and determine whether or not they are realistic. Generally, small achievable goals are much more helpful than larger, more abstract goals. Asking questions such as, "What is the first small step that will let you know you are on the road to recovery?" or "What do you think your (friends, boss, significant other, etc.) will notice about you as you heal more and more?" can help clients identify appropriate treatment goals (Dolan, 1991).

EVALUATING THERAPY

Both clients and therapists need a means of evaluating the therapeutic process. When questioned about whether they use formal or informal methods to evaluate their work, most of the contributors replied that they used informal methods to determine the success of their work. The small number of contributors who routinely used formal evaluation procedures with their clients tended to use standardized psychological tests in a pre/post test format to measure treatment outcomes.

Contributors who use informal methods to evaluate their clients' progress ask their clients for feedback on the therapeutic process. Changes such as a reduction in PTSD symptoms or in trauma-based intrusive memories, increased self-awareness, affective improvements, and cognitive restructuring are used to measure the success of the therapy. Client satisfaction and life changes, achievement of identified goals, and improved work or relationship functioning are other indicators of improvement.

Clinicians who use formal tests need to demystify them with their clients. Tests need to be fully explained to ensure that clients understand their potential usefulness. Informed consent must be obtained prior to testing. The limitations of testing (false negatives or false positives) also need to be discussed, so that clients realize that testing is not an infallible process. Contributors who evaluate their clients with standardized tests use not only scales that have been specifically designed for use with sexual abuse survivors but also other generic psychological tests.

The Dissociative Experiences Scale (DES)—a screening tool to identify survivors with high levels of dissociation—is a self-report test that measures three main factors:

(1) amnestic dissociation;
(2) absorption and imaginative involvement; and
(3) experiences of depersonalization and derealization. (See Appendix C for a copy of the DES.)

The Trauma Symptom Checklist (TSC-33) is a 33-item checklist specifically developed to tap posttraumatic psychological disturbance. The test measures five clinical subscales (dissociation, anxiety, depression, sleep disturbance, and hypothesized post-sexual abuse trauma), as well as developing an overall measure of trauma. This test was developed by John Briere and his colleagues; the TSC-33 is described in Briere's (1989) *Therapy For Adults Molested As Children*. (See Chapter 12.)

The nonabuse-related specific psychological tests that some contributors use to assess and evaluate their clients are the Tennessee Self-Concept Scale, the Beck Depression Inventory, the Hudson Self-Esteem Scale, and the Minnesota Multiphasic Personality Inventory (MMPI).

Some clinicians monitor and evaluate therapy on a regular basis; every fourth or sixth session they will review the process of therapy with their clients. Others evaluate less during the course of therapy, but after termination they make follow-up phone calls to monitor the stability of therapeutic changes. Therapists who work with adolescents will sometimes elicit feedback from their clients' parents or teachers to ascertain whether therapy is being helpful. Group clients sometimes use a peer review process to monitor change and progress. Most clinicians define therapeutic success by items such as increased self-esteem in their clients. Relying on a client's self-assessment in addition to the therapist's own observations of a client's change is generally an adequate basis upon which to evaluate therapy.

Evaluative tools that are easy to administer are an underdeveloped and underutilized resource in clinical work, especially in regard to therapy with abuse survivors. Impressionistic data is the most common form of therapeutic evaluation. As noted above, this method certainly has merit, but it makes generalization from case to case impossible. Improved standardized methods for evaluating therapy are a still-needed resource for therapists working with sexual abuse survivors.

Chapter 5

Individual Therapy: The Victim Phase

This chapter outlines the basic therapeutic tasks during the Victim Phase of therapy. A variety of techniques, some of which are expressive and some of which focus on internal processes, are described. These door-opening interventions are focused on increasing the clients' abilities to become aware of their affective experience, and on developing skills to manage these emotions productively.

The success of psychotherapy in general and abuse-related psychotherapy in particular depends on the nature of the relationship between the therapist and the client. Clients need adequate safety in the relationship to be able to learn and grow. Therapists need sufficient skill and integrity to be able to enhance and support their clients' learning.

As clients develop an awareness of their own psychological processes and make their unconscious responses to trauma conscious, they begin to develop options and choices in how they respond to events in their lives. Dysfunctional patterns that were created to cope with trauma in earlier developmental stages can be replaced by more healthful responses that are appropriate to the client's present life circumstances.

My intention is to give a general map of individual therapy with male survivors, rather than providing a step-by-step guide. I will include specific examples of interventions supplied by the contributors.

The reason that most clinicians suggest male survivors begin with individual work is that an essential feature of abuse-related therapy is safety.

Without sufficient safety, a client cannot address his past history of abuse. If he is focused on here-and-now concerns, he cannot free sufficient psychic energy to address his past.

Individual sessions provide a client with an opportunity to develop familiarity with both his therapist and the therapeutic process. In individual therapy the client is encouraged to speak about his victimization. He is believed and supported. Individual therapy permits a therapist to assess the client's skills and deficits and permits a client to develop a safe relationship with another adult. These two tasks are essential precursors to participation in abuse-focused group therapy.

The focus of early abuse-related therapy is on reclaiming and validating the facts and impacts of the client's victimization. The therapist gives his or her client permission to remember and acknowledge his sexual abuse and listens to his disclosures in a supportive, nonjudgemental manner. The therapist gently questions the client about his past and begins to challenge distorted abuse-generated cognitions that the client has drawn about himself, others, and the world at large.

During this stage of therapy, the therapist works with the client to ensure that therapy is a safe process; this may require teaching the client containment skills (e.g., techniques for managing flashbacks or anxiety attacks) and expanding his understanding of abuse-related processes by the sharing of psychoeducational materials.

The client's behaviors are normalized and destigmatized. He is encouraged to openly examine his abuse experience and its subsequent impacts on him. He is helped to befriend parts of his experience and parts of himself that he has felt ashamed of or pushed away. You can often facilitate this process by the use of gentle humor. For example, challenging self-blaming cognitions by saying, "Oh, there's that old 'I'm-in-charge-of-the-world' part of you again" can help a client recognize dysfunctional aspects of himself without increasing his shame or anxiety.

INTERVENTIONS

Here are some interventions that contributors have used in the Victim Phase of therapy to help clients develop their personal safety, enhance their memory recall, and access repressed affect.

I must caution readers who incorporate these interventions into their work to be discriminating about when and with whom they are used. They must ensure that the use of any technique meets their client's need rather than their own. Indiscriminate enthusiasm about new ideas and interventions can lead to their untimely use. In addition, "No technique can replace the mutual respect and stable affirming relationship offered by good generic psychotherapy..." (Briere, 1989, p. 82).

Inner Child Work

During the Victim Phase of therapy, the inner child metaphor can be introduced. Most clients are helped by the discovery that they have several different ego states. In general, the more dissociated the client, the greater the number of his ego states. Recognizing that different ego states can conflict with one another or react separately to the same stimulus can help clients to be more self-accepting and to better understand their own behavior.

When clients begin to see the "child" part of themselves as having been traumatized and mistreated, they open the door for developing self-loving rather than self-hating ways of being. They begin to develop compassion for themselves, a compassion that is experienced regardless of their affective or cognitive state. Gradually, the client is invited to accept responsibility for "reparenting" the parts of himself that were inadequately parented in his childhood; he is reassured that the therapist is available to act as his guide or coach in this process, so that he has sufficient support for the task.

For some men, the inner child metaphor is difficult to accept initially. Being childlike or having childish ways of reacting to situations is seen in a negative light. This rejection of the immature components of self can sometimes be overcome by the use of metaphors of captivity. Likening an abused child to a prisoner of war whose captors used him for their own ends can assist some men to have greater understanding of the situation they were in as children. Acknowledging that even battle-trained soldiers decompensate in situations of captivity can help some victims become less self-blaming and more self-respecting regarding their own responses to having been abused.

Other men can experience compassion for a girl more easily than they can for a boy. These men believe that males should be more resilient to suffering than females, no matter what their age or situation. With such men, retelling the client's own abuse-related history but changing the gender of the victim can elicit the compassionate feelings that they cannot feel on their own behalf. When they express concern on behalf of the fictional girl-victim, they can be reminded that the very same events happened to them and that they also deserve to be treated with compassion.

Visualization

Visualization can be a useful technique for some clients to acquaint themselves with their "inner child." Before leading a client into this type of visualization, ask him to identify "anchors" for his adult self and his present resourcefulness. These adult reminders can be concrete objects, such as the client's wedding ring or some other symbol of his adult status. Should the client become anxious during the visualization, he can recathect his adult self by touching this symbolic object.

Once the client is grounded in his present reality, lead him into a visualization process by asking him to close his eyes and inducing deep relaxation. If the client is not comfortable closing his eyes, instruct him to focus on one spot in the room while paying attention to his breathing and body sensations. Once the client is deeply relaxed, ask him to get in touch with the child he was just before the abuse began. (The age of the child can vary from situation to situation to suit the client's and the therapist's needs.) Or your suggestion can be more generally phrased, for example, "Let a picture of a child come into your mind."

When the client has an image of a child, ask him to enhance it by asking questions such as, "What is the child wearing?" and "What does the child look like?" Ask the child to let the client's adult self know something that is upsetting him or to tell the client's adult self about his state of well-being. Then ask the client to respond to the child. This exchange between the client's adult self and his inner child can be either silent or spoken. It is helpful to call the child by his age-appropriate name. If a client is called Robert but was called "Bobby" at the time of the abuse, his child self should be addressed as Bobby.

When closing the visualization, ask the client's adult self to ensure that the child is feeling safe and protected before leaving the imagery. There may be some imagined action that will have to occur before the child is ready to say good-bye.

At first, many clients have difficulty contacting their inner child. A client may feel self-conscious taking part in a visualization process or may report that his inner child doesn't want any contact because he feels untrusting or afraid. However, if the client is willing to persevere and if you coach him about how to approach an untrusting or fearful child, he will eventually make contact with his child self. When this occurs, the client is often surprised at how this process can stimulate intense feelings and memories and at how powerfully healing it is to learn to parent the child self.

Guided imagery is a powerful tool for helping clients develop their abilities to create safe personal boundaries. Contributors use this technique in a variety of ways. Here are two of them.

"Container" Visualization

Clients often experience intrusive memories or find themselves obsessively thinking about their abuse experiences. Helping them develop an imaginary "container" in which they can place these memories or thoughts, knowing that they will be there whenever they want to recall them, provides relief.

After ensuring that the client is anchored to his present adult status by some concrete anchors, lead him through a progressive muscle relaxation exercise, until he is deeply relaxed physically. When he shows signs of relaxation, such as rhythmic breathing or closed eyes, instruct him to imagine a container, either a real one or one that he creates in the moment, that is very secure and to which only he has access. Invite him to place experiences, such as intrusive memories and recurring thoughts, in this container and to practice taking them in and out of the container at will. Tell him that whenever he chooses, he can use this container to store his thoughts or feelings. He can always retrieve them when he chooses or he can keep them in the container for as long as he wants.

Some therapists use this exercise to close a session during the early stages of therapy. Just before the client leaves the session, lead him into a trance in which he locates his container and tell him: "Leave any thoughts you don't want to be aware of until your next session in your container." Then gradually bring him back into the here-and-now reality of the therapy room. Training clients to use this technique on a regular basis makes it a familiar way of managing intrusive internal experiences. The more this skill is practiced, the more effective it becomes.

"Place of Safety" Visualization

As with the container visualization, begin this exercise by leading the client through a progressive relaxation exercise until he shows signs of deep relaxation. Tell him to take himself to a place, real or imagined, where he can be by himself in complete comfort and security. Keep your instructions about locating this place deliberately vague, so that the client's unconscious has the freedom to produce a suitable image for his needs in the moment. Ask your client to fully experience this internal place—to hear, see, smell, taste, and feel what it's like. Ask him to anchor his safe place with a hand posture or a readily available physical object (e.g., a marble or stone). Then, if he feels anxious, instruct him to make the hand posture or feel the stone and to signal all levels of his consciousness that he's relaxing and entering a safe place. Tell him that he can return to this place whenever he chooses—no one else need know when he's doing this. Once the client has firmly established a safe inner sanctuary, you can ask him, in a variation on this visualization, to invite someone he trusts and respects to visit his place of safety. If he wants, he can ask his visitor questions or he can receive affirmations from his guest. At all times, the client must be in charge of his safe place and if he has any resistance to inviting someone else into it, this must be respected.

To close this visualization, ask the client to gradually leave his safe place, return to his body, and, when ready, return to the therapy room. Like the container exercise, this technique becomes more effective if it is practiced frequently and becomes a regular feature of a client's self-care.

Making Assumptions

Clients project their own discomfort in discussing certain aspects of their abuse onto the therapist and they are often reluctant to bring these issues into therapy. To challenge the client's projections, the therapist needs to have a direct, nonjudgemental approach when raising difficult issues. This helps to give the client permission to also be direct. The therapist "makes assumptions" that his client is having certain experiences and then he elicits feedback from the client about the accuracy of his assumptions. For instance, in order to know more about his client's homophobic fears, a therapist might say, "I'm not sure if this is true for you, but many survivors are concerned about the arousal they experienced when they were being abused. What was your experience?" This assumption of a common experience and then questioning to elicit the client's own experience can be generalized to many different issues.

Life Book

Invite survivors to revisit the events of childhood with an adult's eye by creating a "life book." Instruct your client to buy a hardcover lined notebook or scrapbook. The book should be of good quality to reinforce the importance of its contents. Tell your client to assign each page a year, starting with the year of his birth and working up to the present. For each year, ask him to write stories or make notes about himself at that time.

The focus is always on the client—if traumatic events happened to others around him, tell him to write about these events as they affected him. The client should leave space at the bottom of the page or in the margin so that he can add later comments to his life story.

The life book is an active and concrete task that provides a way to organize flashbacks and memories in a nonthreatening manner. It indicates time periods in which memories are blocked or repressed. It helps clients recognize their own survival strengths and it opens the door for reflection on their life experience. Clients can be as imaginative as they wish in how they create and use their life books. When reviewing the life book with each client, ask, "What are you learning about yourself in this process?"

Life Story

A similar, but shorter, exercise is having a client tell you his life story. It is helpful to use a structured format so that the survivor has control of the process. Storytelling needs to be a healing experience, not a retraumatizing one. Ask your client to tell you about his family by drawing a genogram on a white board or by bringing in pictures of family members. Symbolic objects, such as rocks or stones, can be used to represent family members. As the client tells his personal history, assist him to identify the ways that he learned to survive his abuse and to look for themes and patterns in his life.

Drawing the Abuse

This can be an effective intervention for clients who are more comfortable with creative media than they are with talking. Give your client a large pad of paper—the size of the paper evokes childhood responses—and tell him to take the paper home and "draw the abuse." Make it clear that this is not an art exercise, but rather an opportunity for the client to recall and clarify events that happened in his past. Tell him to draw a scene in his life before the abuse occurred and then to draw specific scenes of his abuse, using a comic-strip format. For instance, he can draw a bubble coming out of his head to describe what he was thinking or feeling, or he can put captions under his drawings to explain what is going on in them.

Ask the client to bring his drawings into the next therapy session and question him about the information they contain. Don't interpret the drawings—any interpretation that occurs should be the client's. Often, concretizing the images of his abuse makes them seem more real to the client and brings his memories and feelings into greater awareness. In touching the client's self-portrait, the therapist symbolically touches the client, which can nurture the client in a nonthreatening manner.

Script Recognition

This intervention is relatively common practice for therapists trained in Transactional Analysis (TA) and it is well suited for clients who were intrafamilially sexually abused. Six different ego states are identified and each one is symbolized by a chair or cushion.

The first ego state is the "nurturing parent," who is competent in meeting his or her own needs and acknowledges his or her child's needs as separate from his or her own. The second is the "critical parent," who contaminates his or her interactions with the child by his or her own unmet needs. This parent may be critical and punitive, or smothering and overprotective, and does not listen to the child's expression of his own needs. The third is the "adult," who is the rational, logical ego state. The adult is able to analyze situations and seek out new information or skills to support new directions and growth.

The final three ego states are the "natural child," the "compliant child," and the "rebellious child." The natural child is the source of feelings, spontaneity, and creativity. It also carries the wound of the abuse. The compliant and rebellious child ego states are reactive adaptations to the influence of the critical parent and distortions of the natural child's energy.

Once the ego states have been described and identified, ask the client to sit in the position representing the ego state in which he spent most of his time as a child. The timeframe can be divided into before and after the abuse. Encourage him to talk about his experience of being in this place. Ask him to identify the positions that his father and mother usually occupied and to sit in these respective positions and role-play each parent.

This is generally an intense and useful process for clients. Recognizing family members' scripted roles can be liberating as clients realize their own part in maintaining the script and the options they have to create change. The client's first step in altering these processes to is become clear about the overt and covert messages he absorbed as a child and the dynamics he continues to enact in loyalty to his family.

Focusing Techniques

During a session in which a client is talking about his history of abuse or his current life, suggest that he sit quietly and focus on the sensations that are occurring in his body. Ask him to notice if one body sensation or one feeling is particularly noticeable. If he says yes, ask him to really develop his awareness of this sensation. After some time spent in exploring the sensation, ask him if he has any images that come to mind that are connected with the bodily experience he was focusing on. Any images or feelings that surface for the client can be explored and worked with. This technique can help clients retrieve repressed memories and honor their kinesthetic awareness.

The above interventions are samples of the type of work that occurs in the early stages of therapy. As the client becomes more aware of his victimization and, most importantly, of the effects it has had on his life, he begins to move out of the Victim Phase into the Survivor Phase where the therapeutic journey often becomes more intense. When a client stops blaming himself and starts holding the offender accountable for the abuse, he frees up his psychic energy to address the emotions that he has kept out of awareness.

Chapter 6

Individual Therapy: The Survivor Phase

In this chapter, I discuss the middle phase of therapy, the Survivor Phase. During this stage of therapy, the client reclaims dissociated parts of the self (behavior, cognition, and/or affect) and develops new options for handling current life stressors and past traumatic events. I present interventions that increase survivors' affective range and describe ways in which abuse-reactive patterns of interacting with the self and others can be replaced by healthier coping strategies.

The middle phase of therapy, the Survivor Phase, is generally the longest and most difficult. During this phase, the client is challenged to identify where, in his current life, he continues to act out the effects of his victimization. He is then assisted in developing more adaptive living strategies. The client's key task at this stage is to rehearse and internalize new behaviors and beliefs to replace the dysfunctional patterns he has unconsciously developed as a result of his victimization. Generally, the client also engages in abreactive and regressive work during this phase of therapy. These processes unlock repressed emotions and, when well orchestrated, allow the client to integrate previously undigested psychic material.

By the time a client enters the Survivor Phase of therapy, his relationship with his therapist will have matured, permitting him to take greater risks in the therapy process. Consequently, difficult tasks such as working with the client's internalized abuser can be addressed in this phase. The intensity of this stage of therapy can be taxing for both client and therapist. Both parties need to have adequate self-care skills to ensure that their stamina and motivation are sustained throughout this often difficult time.

In this chapter I'll discuss several key therapeutic themes that emerge in the Survivor Phase of therapy:

- working with revenge;
- perpetration and sexual fantasies;
- working with addictive and compulsive processes;
- working to increase clients' affective range; and
- working with dissociative processes.

REVENGE, PERPETRATION, AND SEXUAL FANTASIES

Your clients' fantasies contain important data about their sexual victimization and their reactions to it. The therapeutic relationship must provide opportunities to talk about these fantasies in a nonshaming manner. However, survivors are often reluctant to disclose these fantasies because they feel ashamed of them or are afraid of being judged.

Revenge Fantasies

Most sexually abused men have active revenge fantasies in which they imagine getting even with their abuser. Generally, when asked about their revenge fantasies, clients will reveal their most innocuous fantasy first, until they know they are safe to share more information. Clients need to be supported when revealing their fantasies. They need to know that when fantasies are owned and spoken about rather than kept a secret, they are less likely to be enacted.

Revenge fantasies expose the client's rage and anger. It can be helpful to suggest that the client draw or symbolically act out his fantasy in therapy, while simultaneously discharging his rageful emotions. One symbolic enactment that has proven effective is to cover an old cardboard box with reminders of the abuser and the abuse and then to destroy it. This can occur either in the therapy session or under other circumstances. However, the process should be shared with at least one supportive companion so that the client knows that his anger at his abuser is neither shameful nor secretive.

Whenever a client reveals previously hidden fantasies, he needs to debrief both the content of the fantasy and the process of disclosure. Subsequent to disclosing their fantasies, many clients feel very ashamed of having exposed their private fantasy to their therapist. They may become self-punishing or self-harming if they do not have sufficient internal permission to express these feelings and fantasies. Therapists need to be alert to these dynamics and to ensure that their clients have adequate self-care skills to participate in emotionally intense interventions. Clinicians may frequently need to remind their clients of the difference between fantasy and actual behavior so that their fantasies can be acknowledged and worked with during the therapeutic process.

PERPETRATION AND DEVIANT SEXUAL FANTASIES

If a survivor has perpetrated against another person, he must be held accountable for his behavior and take responsibility for having offended. He should feel appropriate guilt for this behavior while simultaneously contextualizing it in relation to his own victimization so that he can own his behavior in a nonshaming way. If a survivor's offenses are recent or indicate a repetitive pattern, his recovery process will be prolonged while he engages in therapy focused on his offending issues.

Although many survivors have never offended against another person, they may have fantasies in which they imagine themselves abusing a child. Some survivors are very fearful that they may become sexual with a child and they are anxious about these deviant thoughts.

To address this issue, a therapist will need to help the client understand where his fears of becoming a perpetrator originate. For some clients, they stem from an overidentification with the perpetrator (e.g., "I'm like my father, therefore I'll abuse others, too"). For other clients, they are based on having developed "contaminated" sexual arousal patterns during the abuse experience. Having been aroused during his victimization, the client has created masturbatory fantasies which are based on this experience. His subsequent sexual arousal becomes intertwined with abuse-related fantasies.

To address the client's fears of perpetration, the therapist may need to teach cognitive techniques such as thought stopping, so that the client can control his fear-related thoughts or deviant fantasies. If a client has used abuse-related fantasies to reinforce his sexual arousal, he will need to develop other, more appropriate fantasies.

The client will also need to reality-test his fears. He needs to examine his current adult life to look for signs that indicate a propensity to abuse children. Generally, there are none. The therapist may need to remind him that he has ways of meeting his needs as an adult that were not available to him as a child (e.g., he can express his anger or his need to feel powerful, directly, without harming others). If the client's fears persist, he can develop with his therapist a plan to put into place should he begin to exhibit problematic behaviors. Developing a contingency "safety plan" is generally very reassuring to clients who are afraid that they may behave destructively.

CHALLENGING COMPULSIVE/ADDICTIVE BEHAVIORS

Alcohol, drug, food, and sexual addictions are common among abused men, as are other compulsive behaviors such as overworking or compulsive exercising. Therapists must be careful not to focus on the addictive symptoms at the expense of the underlying issues that the addictive behavior was developed to mask.

Addictions serve many purposes. They can be a means of meeting needs that are otherwise not being met or they can be a way to create a distraction in order to avoid acknowledging certain feelings or awarenesses. People develop addictive behaviors because, at least in the short run, they help them cope with experiences they have inadequate skills to address.

In order to change addictive processes, a client has to understand the emotions that drive his behavior and he must be willing to recognize the cost of his addictions in his life. He must be willing to experiment with different options for addressing the unmet needs that have maintained his compulsive behavior.

Therapists must be careful not to engage in a power struggle with an addicted client. A client must be invested in changing his compulsive behavior if he intends to develop alternative coping mechanisms. If the therapist is more invested in this change than his or her client, the therapist will become frustrated. The therapist must always be aware that only the client has the power to change his behavior.

Many therapists recommend that their addicted clients attend appropriate 12-step programs; these groups offer support, information, and a predictable structure that can greatly enhance a client's progress in managing his addictive patterns. Towards this end, therapists must keep themselves informed about 12-step self-help recovery and maintain connections with their local 12-step fellowships.

As the client becomes aware of the state of mind, or feelings, that he has been blocking with his compulsive behavior, he needs support to tackle them directly and develop healthy alternatives for self-care. Often a client will have an abreactive experience as he lets himself feel the affect that he has been blocking with his addictive behavior. This abreaction may generate information about the seed of the addiction. This may enable the client, either gradually or suddenly, to come to terms with the previously unacceptable state of mind or feeling.

INCREASING AFFECTIVE EXPRESSION

Many male survivors have difficulty contacting their feelings. They equate the expression of emotion with vulnerability and powerlessness. Men often believe that they can rely on their physical strength to protect themselves from feeling fearful or vulnerable. Some victims have an inner monologue that says, "If someone were to try to victimize me now, I'd show them who's in charge." These men cover their vulnerability with a display of power. They may become angry with therapists who suggest that they will benefit from befriending their vulnerability. In their minds, they believe these therapists are asking them to become powerless and to risk being revictimized.

Other survivors fear that if they open the door to the expression of their feelings, they will be flooded by uncontrolled affect.

Because repressed emotions are often quite powerful, and, given that the survivor equates feelings with (in some sense) nonsurvival, the former abuse victim may actually believe that emotional release is dangerous. (Briere, 1989, p. 86)

It is important that therapists do not push their clients into affective expression before they are ready. To do so would be counterproductive because it invites resistance and creates a power struggle. Entering intense emotions too quickly may scare some clients away from therapy. Expressing repressed emotions is a natural outcome of the healing process. Therapists and clients must trust that a client will know when he is ready to experience his feelings about the abuse directly.

For some clients, strong emotional release will not be a necessary aspect of their healing. For others, especially those who are unconsciously acting out their emotions in their current relationships, active expressive work will be crucial for them to make the link between their repressed emotions and their current behavior.

Whenever intense affective work or abreactive work occurs in therapy, it is important that it be structured in ways that increase the client's power and mastery. Recreating the original trauma without making therapeutic gains is countertherapeutic for the client.

Clients need to be taught skills for identifying and handling their emotional processes. Many somatic experiences, such as migraine headaches or chronic back pain, cover unexpressed emotions. As the client develops his full capacity to express his emotions, his physical complaints diminish. Leehan and Wilson (1985) state that many former abuse victims have so effectively blocked feelings out of their lives that they do not even know they are having them. Often clinicians need to ask "Do you feel tension in your shoulders? Knots in your stomach? Do you get headaches?" Once such physiological reactions have been identified, you can discuss their meaning and their possible relationship to specific emotions.

Many survivors experience their emotional lives in an all-or-nothing manner. They either block their feelings and push them out of their awareness or they let them explode and are overwhelmed by them. Until clients learn healthy affective containment skills and develop functional ways of expressing feelings, they are likely to continue all-or-nothing emotional response patterns. Predicting this likelihood can motivate clients to manage their emotional inconsistencies as they develop healthier patterns of emotional self-care.

Many clients need support in developing a vocabulary for identifying their different emotions. Therapists can teach clients that their emotions are on a continuum and that they can have varying degrees of fear, anger, joy, and sadness. Clients can be asked to become keen observers of others to see how different people express their emotions. The therapist can often reintroduce lost feelings to the client by making statements such as, "I'm making an assumption that you are feeling some sadness (*or anger or whatever*) about what you're telling me."

Personal and cultural injunctions that limit men's expression of feeling can be identified and challenged. Parental injunctions such as, "Stop crying or I'll give you something to cry about" need to be identified. Often, parts of a client are still loyal to these old messages and until they are brought to consciousness they continue to shape his behavior. Social prescriptions about male emotional expression can be deconstructed by questions such as, "What are men taught in this culture about handling their feelings?" and "What messages are men given about being vulnerable?" and "Do the messages that you've taken in from society about how men should express emotions fit for you and your life?" By challenging these outdated injunctions you give clients new permission to acknowledge their full range of feelings.

Anger is a feeling that most men have cultural permission to express; it often becomes a unidimensional expression of feeling that consumes all other emotions. Other emotions, such as fear or sadness, can become distorted into anger and rage. In order to discover the feelings that underlie their anger, clients must first be helped to fully experience their angry feelings. For this to happen, men need to make a clear distinction between anger and violence. Permission to feel and express anger must never be confused with permission to behave violently.

Usually, survivors find that the emotion they most need to express is not the anger they are feeling, but the fear or another underlying feeling (such as profound sadness) that has been hidden by this mask of anger. Separating primary and secondary feeling processes is part of the therapeutic journey in the survivor phase. For example, when a survivor begins to realize that he gets into fights with others when he is trying to avoid feeling fearful, he can begin to address his fear directly.

For men who are very afraid of uncovering their emotional responses, creating distance from the intensity of their feelings can, paradoxically, help them to contact their affect. Asking men to talk about their feelings in the third person, as if they were talking about a good friend, can help them reclaim this aspect of their lives.

If survivors have very ambivalent feelings, such as feeling both intense love and intense rage at their abuser, therapists must be careful to support both these emotions. Premature efforts towards integration of ambivalence can slow the course of healing. Although the client may be frustrated by the apparently contrary feelings that he experiences, both his conflicting emotions speak to his emotional truth, and both must be honored. Many abused clients need to learn that both love and anger can be felt simultaneously and that the two feelings are not mutually exclusive.

Since the repressed or disowned feelings that survivors bring into therapy are based on past experience, it is helpful for the therapist to suggest future possibilities to the client to help him change his present emotional patterns. Talking about a future in which the client feels emotionally integrated and his feelings are in harmony with his thoughts and behaviors can seed the expectation that these are achievable goals for the client to work towards.

Contributors have used a variety of techniques to assist their clients to increase their affective expression. Some use *music* to elicit their client's feelings, playing a love song during a session and asking the client to imagine singing it to himself. This exercise may reveal resistance to loving oneself or cynicism about the concept of love. Whatever specific response emerges, it will be a doorway to further exploration of affective responses.

The gestalt *empty chair* technique is a method that some contributors use to assist their clients to discover their feeling responses. Clients who are concrete and practical in their orientation may have difficulty engaging in this type of activity. Clients who are willing to participate in this intervention can have their entry into the exercise "primed" by their *writing a letter* to the person or the part of themselves that they want to put in the empty chair. They can then start the dialogue by reading this letter out loud. It is important that clients understand that the letters they write in therapy are not intended to be sent to the actual person to whom they are addressed; rather they are directed to the internalized image of that person which the client carries in his mind.

Clients who are comfortable with nonverbal media can be asked to *construct a collage* to show what it feels like to be victimized, angry, or grieving. During the process of making the collage, or while it is being discussed in therapy, the client will generally contact the affect associated with the events shown in the collage.

Some contributors use *breathwork* as an intervention in emotional release. Increasing the frequency of the breathing pattern, as in holotropic breathwork, can encourage a client to regress. Therapists who use these types of techniques require considerable training in them before they can use them expertly.

Less technical forms of breathwork can occur that assist survivors to develop skills to manage their emotions. Clients can be asked to become aware of their breath while they are focused on a train of associative events that elicit emotional responses. This ensures that they do not start to hold their breath as the intensity of feeling increases. Clients can be coached to send their breath to a particular part of their body or to give a sound to their breath in order to shift their emotional awareness to a deeper level. The suggestion that a client let his breath carry out the feelings that are flooding him as he remembers a traumatic memory can give a survivor a new option of being able to hold the memory in his awareness without being traumatized by it. Practicing breathing techniques that induce physical relaxation gives a client confidence that he can be present with his memories of the abuse without being overwhelmed by them.

Various forms of *emotionally expressive work* are used by contributors to support their clients' affective growth. The purpose of this kind of work is to recathect the original feelings that were dissociated during the abuse and to externalize them in concrete form so that clients can increase their comfort with, or reduce their fear of, these emotions. For instance, if a client is feeling loss and sadness about his lack of self-esteem, he can be asked to engage in a tug-of-war (using a towel or some other suitable prop) to take back his self-esteem. During the tug-of-war, coach the client to verbalize and vocalize his anger at having his self-esteem damaged by his abuser. Similarly, if a client wants to rid himself of his feelings of sexual shame, he can be helped to construct a way of literally pushing these feelings away from himself. The key in such dramatizations is to be alert for clues and cues from the client that suggest a unique and personal way of concretizing and externalizing feelings and affective processes.

Role-play can be a very effective way to elicit emotions. If a scene from a client's abuse is role-played, it is advisable to subsequently role-play scenes that give the client nurturing and protective messages so that he can develop a supportive and caring inner script. Clients should not be asked to role-play their perpetrators during the survivor phase of therapy. If this is done at all, it should not occur until the thriver phase. If a client plays his perpetrator before he has thoroughly addressed his own emotional reactions to the abuse, he can become too aware of the offender's vulnerabilities and prematurely forgive his perpetrator without fully exploring his own emotional processes.

Bioenergetic anger releases are used by some contributors to help clients find a powerful, but safe, outlet for their rage. Therapists must ensure that prior to engaging in this type of intervention they make a contract with their clients to stop this work should either the therapist or the client become concerned about the direction it starts to take. Therapists need to be familiar with this type of work so that they are emotionally available to the client during the emotional release and not preoccupied with their own reaction to the client's intense feelings. Clients who engage in anger-focused work need to be coached to keep their eyes open and feet firmly grounded so that they don't move into a blind rage. After this kind of work, the client needs to debrief it thoroughly so that he can integrate any new insights gained through the process.

Any props that a therapist needs to support active emotional release work, such as tennis racquets, towels, pillows, and so on, need to be readily available in his or her office. Tactile comforters should also be available so that clients can nurture themselves as needed. Many men are reluctant to pick up a teddy bear or other childish symbol of comfort, but they will use a stuffed basketball or a blanket for the same purpose.

If emotional releases occur in the presence of other people, such as in a group session, the observers need to be warned that the process can trigger their own reactions. They need permission to take care of themselves during the process. For some men, this will mean covering their eyes and ears. Others may need to change their seating arrangement so that they can sit close to someone they trust. The observers will also need time after the emotional release so that they, too, can debrief the experience.

WORKING WITH DISSOCIATIVE PROCESSES

Children are generally honest and forthright, unless they believe that it is not safe for them to tell the truth. When they are told not to talk about something that has happened in their lives, such as being sexually abused, they have to "forget" what has happened in order not to lie. In technical jargon, they learn to dissociate from their behaviors, feelings, sensations, and/or cognitions.

If one likens a child to a house, one can say that a child who is dissociative has closed the door on some rooms in his house and acts as if they do not exist. Memories of being abused are kept behind metaphoric locked doors, blocked from his conscious awareness. The abused-self is, in effect, split off and dissociated from the child's self-identity.

Although an adult survivor may not have conscious memories of the events that he has stored behind locked doors, he may exhibit behaviors that hint at these ghosts. For example, a man who was abused in a basement may have no memory of the abuse, but may become very anxious whenever he has to enter a basement. Some men feel sexually aroused until the point at which the sexual behavior becomes interactive. Although they do not recall being abused, their behavior speaks to the reality of their victimization. Patterns of behavior or thinking and feeling that do not belong in the present circumstances of the survivor's life often indicate the presence of dissociated experiences. In many ways,

...unassimilated trauma...[causes] flashbacks, overreaction to stimuli, distortions of perceptions and high levels of internal stress. (Steele & Colrain, 1991, p. 1)

Dissociative survivors need to educate themselves about their dissociative processes. They must begin to notice when and where they dissociate. *Keeping a journal* by making daily entries that help them to track their dissociative episodes is informative. As clients begin to learn what triggers their dissociative states (i.e., certain times of day, parts of a house, kinds of activities, etc.), they have the option of staying dissociated or developing other ways of dealing with the situation that is stress inducing.

As clients become conscious of their dissociative patterns, they can ask themselves, when finding themselves dissociated, "What part of me is needing to leave now?" Learning *grounding techniques* to bring them back into their present reality and present identity can be helpful to survivors who dissociate. *Looking in a mirror* reminds a client that he is an adult and not a powerless child. Writing about the situation that is eliciting traumatic memories and *writing to or telling someone about the memories* can validate a survivor's experience and reduce his isolation. Keeping *symbols of his adult identity* available can also reconnect a survivor to his current self and break his dissociative state. Some survivors are uncomfortable with these interventions because engaging in them acknowledges their abuse, which can be painful.

The most extreme type of dissociation is MPD. Clients who develop MPD are overdifferentiated and their therapy is focused on assisting them to reintegrate fragmented parts of self (called "alters"). To continue the analogy of a house, clients who have MPD live in many separate rooms, with no corridors to link them together. Therapy needs to help the client reconnect the rooms. MPD is a coping strategy created to deal with abusive situations that are too overwhelming for a child's immature ego to integrate. Although the original intent of the defense was to secure the child's survival, this unconscious coping strategy no longer works well in an adult client's life. Parts of the self are identified with a time that is no longer current and act in ways that are no longer functional. The barriers between the different alters need to be dismantled and the functions that they serve need to be integrated and updated.

In general, if MPD is pathologized, clients tend to act in pathological ways; if MPD is normalized, clients tend to act in normal ways and continue attending school, going to work, and so on. In order for the different parts of the self to fuse, clients need adequate stability in their lives. Therapeutic safety has to be established with all the alter personalities, one at a time, and the specific role of each alter and the information that he or she carries must be brought into awareness.

During the survivor stage of therapy, provided that a client feels secure within the therapeutic alliance and is not consumed with current life crises, dissociated experiences are invited back into conscious awareness. This reclamation is often accompanied by the release of intense repressed emotion. The client temporarily enters an altered state of consciousness and, in effect, relives the incidents that he has dissociated. This process is called abreaction.

Traumatic memories may need to be abreacted several times in order that all the missing pieces be accessed (Steele & Colrain, 1991). A list of changes in behavior that indicate when abreactive work is finished has been developed by Steele and Colrain (1991). These are:

1. The client has a relatively continuous memory of the traumatic time period(s).
2. He is not currently dissociating in an uncontrolled or dysfunctional way.
3. He is not experiencing flashbacks or reliving the trauma in other ways.
4. He can remember and talk about the trauma without intolerable affect.
5. He has developed a subjective sense of the personal meaning of the trauma.
6. He expresses interest in and hope for the future rather than feeling overwhelmed by the past.

Survivors are on a continuum of memory repression. On one end of the continuum are those survivors who have total recall of their abuse; on the other end are those who have no memory of their abuse. The majority of survivors are in between these two poles; they have some conscious memories and some memory gaps. It is not necessary for a survivor to reclaim all, or even most, of his repressed memories in order to heal. Survivors need only have sufficient memory recall to counter their own denial.

When clients are doing abreactive work in therapy, it is often necessary to schedule therapy sessions more frequently to give the client adequate support and safety. Healing occurs when old traumatic memories are revisited and new affective and cognitive associations to them are forged. After successful abuse-related therapy, traumatic memories, when they occur, have a context of powerful new associations. The client has a new context and new skills for processing his past experience. For instance, a new association is made when a therapist witnesses a client's abreaction, so that the abuse memory no longer connotes isolation and shame. Another new association occurs when a client has permission to fully express the feelings that his abuse memory invokes without having to temper their expression to meet other people's (i.e., the abuser's) needs.

(For more information about working with abreactive processes, see Steele and Colrain's excellent chapter on "Abreactive work with sexual abuse survivors: Concepts and techniques" in *The Sexually Abused Male, Volume 2* (Hunter, 1990b).)

Therapeutic Dissociation

Therapeutic dissociation, which can also be called trancework or hypnosis, is a powerful tool that can help clients manage their unconscious dissociation. This intervention works paradoxically—unconscious dissociative behaviors developed during the abuse are managed and assimilated in therapy by the use of conscious dissociation.

Trancework in therapy is an extension of a natural process. Daydreaming, highway hypnosis, and systematic relaxation techniques are common trance experiences that are familiar to most clients.

Before you engage in trancework with clients, it is important to educate the client about this kind of intervention. Therapeutic dissociation is a natural process, but often it needs to be normalized and demythologized for clients. Clients can be told that hypnosis is a method of asking the subconscious mind to help the client in his healing journey. The client needs only to remember events that will be helpful to his healing process.

Before he enters a trance, the client is grounded, or anchored, in his present adult reality. This grounding is made in as many representational systems as possible, so that the client can call on all of his senses to assist him to leave the trance, should he wish to do so. Clients are advised that spontaneous age regressions can occur in trance states. This is a normal and common occurrence.

With hypnosis, clients can often connect with thoughts and beliefs that they developed as a child but that are not available to their normal consciousness. If the client has dissociated core negative beliefs that he developed as a child, this information can often be reclaimed during trance states and brought into consciousness. This process is called state-dependent learning. Thought errors and mistaken beliefs can then be challenged by the client's adult mind.

Therapeutic dissociation invites less conscious aspects of the client's mind to support his conscious mind in actively creating change. It helps the client gain mastery over processes he has previously used in unconscious and dysfunctional ways. As abuse survivors become skillful at entering trance states at will, they begin to notice the times in their lives when they unconsciously enter a trance state. This new awareness brings an opportunity to develop more functional methods of addressing stressful situations in their present reality.

Two specific therapeutic dissociation interventions originally developed by Yvonne Dolan are presented in Appendix D (see page 177). One intervention helps clients in a dissociated state to ground themselves; it is also an effective induction for physical relaxation. The second intervention provides survivors with a format for processing flashbacks and clarifying which aspects of their present reality they perceive as threatening.

Contributors agreed that therapeutic dissociation is a very useful tool to help clients manage their traumatic memories, but less useful as a method of recalling repressed memories. Clients who recall lost memories under hypnotic suggestion often don't feel confident that the memories are valid. The contributors also agreed that therapists who intend to use hypnosis with their clients must obtain adequate training and supervision in this work.

Therapeutic dissociation is not a suitable intervention for clients whose motivation to use hypnosis is nontherapeutic (e.g., a client who is not really interested in working through his abuse, but wants more information with which to blame others for making his life miserable). It is also not advisable to use this type of intervention with clients who are psychotic or with clients who are taking legal action against their perpetrator. The reason for this latter prohibition is that hypnotically recalled memories are not permissible evidence in court and a client could risk losing his case on this technicality.

Chapter 7

Individual Therapy: The Thriver Phase

With a few exceptions, such as when an abused client either symbolically or actually confronts his abuser(s), many of the issues addressed in this final phase of therapy are the same as those addressed with clients who haven't been sexually abused. I discuss the usefulness and appropriateness of body-focused therapy in this stage of treatment for some clients. Finally, I address the termination of abuse-focused therapy and make suggestions for ensuring the sucess of this transition.

By the time a client enters the thriver phase of therapy, most of the work that occurs in therapy sessions is similar to that conducted with non-abused clients. The hardest part of the client's healing journey is generally completed by this stage.

Often, this phase is a satisfying and enjoyable time for both the client and the therapist; dysfunctional abuse-created patterns have been replaced with healthier ones, and the client's self esteem is dramatically increased.

Issues typically brought into therapy by thrivers focus on relational difficulties with their partners, children, or extended family; sexual difficulties and dysfunctions; and personal safety and self-care concerns (Courtois, 1991). Typically, therapy to address these issues is no different for clients who have been sexually abused than for other clients.

By this stage of therapy, clients should be able to identify and manage their personal boundaries. Some clients choose to engage in body-focused therapies in this stage of their recovery, a task for which they should by now be sufficiently prepared.

For some survivors, body-focused therapy techniques reach wounds that would otherwise be overlooked. Body-focused therapies directly raise issues that are central to survivors' sense of safety, such as their degree of comfort with their bodies and with touching and being touched. This chapter discusses these issues in greater detail in a section called "Body-work."

CONFRONTING THE ABUSER

One piece of therapeutic work that belongs in the thriver stage and is unique to sexually abused clients is the need to fully reclaim their personal power. One can encourage this by having the client confront his abuser, either symbolically or, in a few cases, in person. In cases of intrafamilial abuse, some clients express a desire to confront several members of their extended family. A client's family is involved only if his safety is not jeopardized by such a plan. Which family members are invited to sessions focused on confrontation depends upon their readiness to attend, the nature of the client's current relationship with them, and the nature of his relationship with them in the past.

Before a confrontation session can take place, a client must be completely confident of his own childhood memories and experiences. Whether a family meeting is real or symbolic, several sessions need to be used to prepare for it. The therapist must ensure that the client's expectations for the confrontation session are realistic and achievable. Possible outcomes of the session must be predicted and strategies that support the client must be developed for every eventuality. The key to successful confrontation is the client's definition of his goals. Goals need to be stated in such a way that achieving them depends on the client's own process, not on any desired response from others.

For some clients, family sessions are disappointing. Their secret wish that if they speak about the problems in the family these problems will be cured is shattered. Family members may react to information about the client's abuse with denial, minimization, or rationalization. If the client is not adequately prepared for these eventualities, he can be very upset.

Other clients find family sessions very confirming, whether or not they progress smoothly. The opportunity to reality-test beliefs about family members can be affirming as the client witnesses their predictable behavior patterns. Seeing his own growth and acknowledging his ability to differentiate from his family can be empowering. Sometimes a client's previous beliefs about his family are disconfirmed and he finds that he can see his family more realistically.

BODYWORK

Information and memory about abuse are held not only in the survivor's mind but also in his body. Some clients find that as part of their recovery process they need to augment traditional psychotherapy with nonverbal, body-focused therapies. They intuitively realize that the trauma that occurred to their bodies needs to be addressed by physical as well as by symbolic interventions for their full recovery.

Bodywork consists of a continuum of interventions ranging from those in which the client is fully dressed and no physical touch occurs through breathwork and yoga-like stretches to full massage. The types of healing processes that can occur as a result of bodywork are myriad. They can be both physiological and psychological. A trained bodyworker must be skilful in both physical process therapy and psychological therapy. It is quite common for survivors to reclaim abuse-related memories during bodywork. A trained bodyworker should be prepared to assist his or her clients to work through abreactions should they occur.

A physiological benefit of bodywork is that it helps clients to become aware of any chronic unconscious physical tension that they have developed as a defense structure. The body's defense systems are unconsciously controlled. As a result of chronic nervous tension, muscle fascia can become locked into defensive body armoring. Bodywork helps clients become aware of these areas of chronic tension. This opens opportunities to create change as they learn to relax and discharge repressed affect.

The trauma of abuse often causes psychosomatic responses that unbalance the nervous system. Overactive nerve stimulation results in hypertonic reactions such as extreme tension and an inability to relax. On the other hand, hypotonic reactions result in depression and lethargy. Therapists can train survivors in relaxation techniques and assist them to experience deeper and deeper levels of relaxation, gradually restructuring both their emotional and physical responses.

Psychologically, bodywork has many benefits for survivors. Working with a trained bodyworker may be the first time that a survivor negotiates safe, contractual touch with another person. Bodywork is an opportunity to practice receiving nurturing, nonsexual touch in which the client controls the type of contact he receives. This lets the client experience and define his own autonomous physical boundaries.

Many abuse survivors have either avoided physical contact with others or been hypersexualized and had indiscriminate physical contact. In either case, they have experienced little real choice about the degree of touch they receive and the circumstances under which it is obtained. Learning to determine the type of touch they desire by responding to internally defined needs can be very important. Bodywork can be the circumstance under which this learning takes place.

Many abuse survivors have distorted images of their bodies or they have developed an avoidant relationship with their physical selves. Some survivors feel very marginally connected to their bodies. Others experience great discomfort with their bodies or their body processes. Bodywork can help clients to reclaim and reconnect with their bodies on their own terms. Many clients begin to *feel* their feelings for the first time as previously dissociated physical sensations and processes are brought into awareness.

Whether or not to engage in bodywork must always be the client's decision. The therapist should not raise the possibility of bodywork until the client himself indicates an awareness of the physical aspects of his abuse-related experience. If a client feels too threatened by bodywork, he will not follow through on any suggestions to pursue this option.

With some exceptions, the bodyworker and the psychotherapist should generally be two different people to reduce the possibility of developing negative transference in the psychotherapeutic process. This separation of roles gives the client an opportunity to process his experience in bodyfocused therapy or any transference reactions he may have to the bodyworker, with a neutral and supportive third party, namely, his therapist. An exception to these dual roles for the therapist and the bodyworker occurs when bodywork takes place in a group setting and the psychotherapist is not alone with the client.

As discussed previously, touch boundaries need to be very carefully observed in psychotherapy. When a therapist has developed a relationship with a client and the client subsequently expresses interest in bodywork, a psychotherapist who begins to work physically with the client can be seen as inviting the client to repeat the original abuse dynamic. The client may see the work that has occurred in therapy prior to the bodywork as an elaborate grooming process. The client's belief that authority figures will eventually attempt to become physical or sexual with him is reconfirmed.

Although the two people who provide psychotherapy and bodywork should be distinct individuals, their work needs to be connected. Clients who are working with more than one therapist must be asked to give consent for information to be shared between the various service providers to ensure that the client receives the best possible treatment. Working with more than one professional can lead to their roles being unproductively split or insufficient information being shared among all the parties.

Clients who have active addictions or suffer from psychotic breaks are not candidates for bodywork. Neither are clients who have unrealistic or inappropriate expectations about the bodywork process. Some clients who have little memory of their abuse engage in bodywork because they assume that this will unlock their repressed memories. Although this may occur, there is no guarantee that it will. Clients may end up dismissing the usefulness of bodywork, not because it couldn't help them but because it did not conform to their expectations.

If a client decides to engage in bodywork, it is advisable for him to ask his therapist, or other survivors or clinicians, for a referral to a bodyworker who has experience working with abuse survivors. He should also rely on his intuitive responses; if he does not feel comfortable with a bodyworker he should not work with him or her. A client's first meeting with a bodyworker should focus on building a working contract focused on the issues the client brings to this type of therapy. The bodyworker needs to assess the client's needs and determine if they are appropriate for his or her practice. Although the bodyworker should not intrusively question the client about his abuse, he or she needs to gather sufficient information to ensure that his or her interventions are appropriate. Asking the client to "Tell me only what I need to know about your abuse history in order to help you heal" ensures that the client has control over what he does or does not choose to disclose.

The bodyworker should explicitly tell the client that sexual touch or sexual stimulation will not be a part of their relationship. He or she should also inform the client that should the client experience sexual feelings during the session, the client should signal the bodyworker and they will renegotiate the work they are doing together. At all times, the client must be in charge of the kind of contact he has with the bodyworker and he must be able to stop the process whenever he chooses.

A skillful bodyworker will always ask the client's permission before proceeding with any form of physical contact. If the bodyworker notices any nonverbal client discomfort, he or she should say, "I see you tense up when I approach your shoulder (or another body part). Do you want me to continue? How would you like me to touch you there?" The client's feedback should always guide the kind of work that the bodyworker does.

It is important that bodywork occur in a forum in which the highest ethical standards prevail. Both the potential for revictimization and the potential for more complete recovery are present when a survivor decides to pursue nonverbal therapy. A bodyworker must operate with a very high degree of integrity to ensure that the process of bodywork is safe and healing.

Concerns about possible sexual implications of touch have caused many psychotherapists to avoid bodywork altogether. The solution is professional growth and education, not avoidance. (Timms & Connors, 1990, p. 130)

TERMINATION

The final step of therapy for a thriver is to plan the termination of his therapy. This final task deserves the same thoughtful consideration that was given to all previous therapeutic tasks. Celebrating a client's successes and acknowledging his ongoing skills and strengths are part of this final process. A thorough review of the client's therapeutic progress and an open acknowledgement of the importance of the therapeutic relationship to both the client and the therapist are essential. The client should leave therapy cleanly without any unresolved issues or unfinished business about the therapeutic process itself.

Clients indicate their readiness for termination by consistently behaving in self-supporting ways that indicate that they are ready to become the architects of their own recovery. This does not necessarily mean that they no longer exhibit abuse-related symptoms; however, when such symptoms are present, the client feels confident and capable in addressing them.

It is important that the client who is terminating knows that the therapist's door is open should he need to return. Some clients are reassured by infrequent check-ups with the therapist and use irregularly scheduled follow-up sessions to stabilize their therapeutic gains. Other clients need to know that they can reestablish therapeutic support without any loss of face or shame if unexpected events occur, such as recalling previously repressed abuse memories. Leaving the client with an option of renewing his contract with the therapist, should the need arise, creates safety within the termination process.

Chapter 8

Group Therapy with Male Survivors of Sexual Abuse

This chapter describes a two-stage group process for adult male survivors. Screening criteria and general ground rules for the group are presented. The psychoeducational focus of the first-stage group and the process-focused nature of the second-stage group are described and differentiated. I recommend a co-leadership model of group facilitation and discuss issues relating to the gender of the leaders.

Individual therapy provides male survivors with a safe and supportive forum where they can identify and examine their abuse-related history. An individual therapist is often the first person whom a survivor has entrusted with information about his childhood sexual abuse and how he subsequently handled this experience. Although individual therapy has a central place to play in the recovery process, it is enhanced and complimented by group treatment.

Abuse-focused group therapy provides survivors with opportunities to normalize their experiences and reduce their isolation. Many adult survivors are empowered by the realization that they were not alone in having been abused by a trusted adult. Survivor groups provide clients with an opportunity to experience a social milieu where respect for personal boundaries is paramount and they can practice new skills for relating to the self and others. Group members model healing for one another and catalyze each others' growth.

Male survivor groups assist their members by providing a safe, structured, and nurturing environment in which to learn new skills and resolve the trauma of sexual abuse. For many survivors, this is the first opportunity they have ever had to talk with other men about having been vulnerable and hurt. A survivor who joins a survivors' group is openly declaring that he was abused. Joining a group is a tangible sign that his denial is over and he is willing to work with his abuse issues more directly (Timms & Connors, 1990).

The support survivors receive from their fellow group members takes a number of forms. Being listened to and believed is a powerful validation of each survivors' victimization experience. Hearing other members' abuse-related stories often evokes previously repressed feelings of compassion or anger within survivors. Initially, these feelings are projected onto other group members; eventually, they are reclaimed and integrated into the self. Sharing emotionally with other men without this intimacy being fraught with sexual undertones opens new possibilities of male friendship for many survivors.

Group membership gives survivors opportunities to become aware of maladaptive interactive processes and to practice new interpersonal skills. Either by direct interactions with other group members or through role-playing in the group, members learn how to resolve conflict nonviolently, how to get their needs met, and how to give and receive nonsexual affection. Giving as well as receiving help enhances clients' self-esteem and counteracts their sense of powerlessness.

Group members model both effective and ineffective coping strategies for one another. They give each other direct and indirect feedback on many levels. Frequently, group interventions occur indirectly. Group members experience vicarious learning as they witness their peers grow and change. "Each time someone takes more charge of his life, it underscores the reality of recovery for everyone" (Lew, 1988, p. 212).

However, group treatment is not a panacea for all survivors. For some clients, a group experience can be overwhelming. If a client's internal resources are not strong enough to counter the weight of the group process, a group experience can be countertherapeutic. Each client has much less control of his experience in a group than he does in individual therapy. The fact that clients spark one another's memories and catalyze one another's growth can be either positive or negative, depending on each client's readiness.

SCREENING POTENTIAL GROUP MEMBERS

The assessment process for potential group clients sets a tone for subsequent group experiences. Time spent on a thorough and comprehensive assessment is time well invested. In order to obtain useful information, assessment questions need to be direct, concrete, and behavioral.

Group screening serves a function for both client and therapist. Clients can use the assessment interview as an opportunity to find out about group treatment and to gather the information they need to make a decision about whether or not to engage in this process. Clinicians use screening interviews to solicit data about potential clients' abuse histories and their recovery process to date in order to assess their potential readiness for a group experience. During the screening interview, a client is expected to tell the group therapists about his abuse history in sufficient detail for the therapists to have enough information to be able to skillfully facilitate the client's growth in the group. Clients should also receive information about the group's treatment goals, philosophy, and process. It's helpful to give clients handouts about the group, such as a list of acceptable and unacceptable behaviors in the group, or information about the group's purpose and structure. (For an example of a list of behaviors that support group process see Appendix E.)

The contributors assess the following specific issues to determine a client's readiness to participate in an abuse-related therapy group.

The Client's Ability to Talk About His Abuse

Survivors must be able to talk about their abuse with some degree of comfort before joining an abuse-related group. They should have at least one clear memory of having been abused. If they can only talk about their abuse as "it," or if they are unable to say or hear words that refer specifically to abusive processes, they are not ready to join a group.

Support

Clients who have no supports outside of the therapy group are not good candidates for group treatment. A group member should have access to at least one close friend or a 12-step support network to supply social support outside of the group. Ideally a client engaged in group treatment should also be engaged in concurrent individual therapy, at least on an as-needed basis. Group therapists should obtain a release of information from clients during the assessment process, so that they have permission to contact the client's individual therapist if necessary.

In some situations, a shortage of suitable individual therapists or a client's lack of financial resources may rule out the possibility of concurrent individual therapy. In such cases, before admitting a client to their group, the leaders need to be very sure that the client's self-care skills and social supports are sufficient to meet the demands of group membership.

Motivation

Group clients should be able to discuss how their sexual victimization is currently a problem in their lives. They should also be able to articulate desired goals they intend to work toward during the group process. If clients are referred to group treatment by their individual therapist, it is important to ensure that the interest in group therapy belongs to the client and not to his therapist. Clients who attend a group because someone else thinks they should are not good candidates for group treatment.

Interpersonal Skills

Group members need to have adequate interpersonal skills to be able to participate in a group. A client who is scapegoated by other group members because of poor social skills is only revictimized or patronized by group treatment. Until such time as a client has sufficient social skills to fully participate in a group, he is better served by other treatment modalities.

Self-Care

Potential group members should be able to describe self-care strategies to deal with both their own pain and the pain of listening to others. They must demonstrate that they not only are aware of such strategies, but actually put them into practice.

Homophobia

Actively homophobic clients are not well-suited to abuse-related group treatment. Abused men need to have space to explore their sexual orientation and masculine identity during group treatment and adamantly heterosexist attitudes curtail this exploration.

Both gay and straight men are treated in the same abuse-focused groups. Some contributors said that they used to separate groups into gay and straight, but noted that they no longer observe this practice. The focus in male survivor group treatment is on the common human experience of having been abused, not on the issue of sexual orientation.

Contributors discussed a paradox: although many male survivors are very concerned about the implications of having been abused by a man (if their perpetrator was male) and many of them are quite homophobic, they have a strong desire to establish closer relationships with men. They noted that having both gay and straight men in a group initially causes consternation. At first, the men are very sensitive to each other's sexual orientation, as they establish their own comfort in the group. However, when clients come to know one another, and to understand the differences between pedophiles and homosexuals, this tension eases. By the end of the group, sexual orientation has become an irrelevant issue as the group members open up to one another and share their humanity.

Present-Life Functioning

Clients who are actively addicted or very recently recovered addicts are not suitable candidates for group treatment. Suicidal or homicidal clients are too emotionally unstable to join a group. Clients currently in physically or sexually abusive relationships need to address these issues directly before they enter a survivors' group. A client who is actively psychotic or currently processing a major life crisis is not a candidate for group treatment.

Abuse-Reactive Perpetration

Therapists must ask clients if they have engaged in abuse-reactive perpetration. You will have to determine how to evaluate acts of abuse that happened when a client was an adolescent. A general rule of thumb is that a client who has committed any patterned, repetitive acts of perpetration, or who has committed acts of perpetration in the last five years, is disqualified from participating in a survivors' group.

MPD

Clients who have MPD can be suitable group members, provided they have sufficient control of their various alter personalities. Clients who can develop therapeutic contracts about how they manage their dissociation and who can ensure that their persecutor alters will not be brought into the group, can be group members. The group therapists need to educate the other group members about MPD and the process of splitting into alter personalities, in order to normalize this process.

A TWO-STAGE GROUP TREATMENT MODEL

The contributors have developed a variety of group models to work with sexually abused males: single-leader groups, dual-leader groups, structured and unstructured groups, and open and closed groups are all offered by different therapists in different locations. Some of these models are based on theoretical principles, others are based on practical necessities. However, whether or not they facilitated a group themselves, all the contributors agreed on the usefulness of group treatment. The group treatment model presented here reflects both the contributors' experiences with group therapy and my own.

I recommend a two-stage group process. The first stage is a closed, structured eight-to-ten-week psychoeducational group, which suits clients who are in the victim phase of therapy. Clients who wish to pursue group treatment further are well served by a second stage—an open-ended, unstructured group, which focuses on resolving abuse-related trauma and developing functional life skills. The level of processing and the intensity of this second-stage group are suited to clients in the survivor phase of therapy.

There are many reasons why this model is suitable for survivors of sexual abuse. As with individual therapy, safety is the guiding principle when one is offering group treatment to survivors. Initially, when survivors begin to attend an abuse-focused group, they are nervous and hesitant. They feel anxious about discussing their victimization with others. A structured psychoeducational group, in which the group itinerary is known in advance, is a safe entry into unfamiliar group process.

Each week, the psychoeducational group focuses on a selected theme, such as sexuality, coping strategies, self-care, abuse dynamics, and so on. Clients are given written materials before each group or exercises that they are asked to complete prior to the group session. The leader tells clients to ask for time in the group to address their personal concerns on an "as-needed" basis. However, no one expects any group member to self-disclose unless he chooses to do so.

All the clients in the psychoeducational group begin the group and end the group at the same time. This structure provides newcomers to group therapy with an equal opportunity to develop safe and predictable relationships in a group context. It also means that the group members move through the various stages of group development on the same schedule. The initial session focuses on group rules and procedures, the middle sessions focus on abuse-related material and developing group process, and the final session acts as a celebration of growth and sharing.

This gentle entry into abuse-focused material supports and empowers clients. It also provides the therapists with an opportunity to fully assess the group members' capacity to handle group process within a contained structure. The psychoeducational group permits clients who are not yet ready to move into a more intense process-focused group to successfully complete a group experience. They can then concentrate on enhancing their skills until they're fully prepared to continue in a process group.

The second-stage group is more demanding of both clients and therapists. This group is unstructured, in the sense that it relies on the clients to generate the material that is addressed each week. It is less predictable for both clients and therapists since the agenda cannot be known in advance. It is also more fluid and more interactive than the psychoeducational group. Clients may be asked to participate in each other's work and they are expected to be active participants in the group process.

The second-stage group is open-ended. This means that clients determine how long they stay in the group based on its usefulness to them. Contributors who run groups for male survivors estimate the average length of time a client stays in a group is generally between one and two years. Because group members have different entry times into the group, the established group members take on the role of enculturating and supporting new members.

Abuse-focused groups are a hybrid of self-help and therapist-led processes. The sharing and support clients offer one another are essential components of recovery. However, at certain times, the therapists' skills in handling abreactive situations or helping clients decode their transference reactions are crucial to clients' healing. Therapists must develop discernment about when to facilitate the group process and when to sit back and let the group members carry the ball.

The groups that contributors work with have from six to ten members. A group with eight members is ideal; however, one or two members more or less will not interfere with the delivery of quality service.

The contributors run their group sessions for differing lengths of time; an hour to an hour and a half was the shortest group session and three hours the longest. I recommend that group sessions be two to two and a half hours in order to give all group members sufficient time to fully engage in the process. Group sessions should be held weekly, although the second-stage process may take several scheduled breaks throughout the year.

This two-stage model recommends that group membership be reserved for male survivors only. I think most survivors, both male and female, initially benefit from working with group members of the same sex with whom they can more easily let shame and embarrassment surface. However, some contributors work with mixed-gender groups and report success with this model. Mixed-gender groups are best reserved for clients who wish to pursue further group therapy after they have completed an all-male second-stage group. A mixed-gender group is best able to help a client who is in the thriver phase of therapy.

GROUP GROUND RULES

Both first and second-stage groups need to develop a set of ground rules to provide safety and structure to the group process. Although many ground rules are common among different groups, each group needs to ensure that it's own ground rules fit its unique identity. Spending time during the first session of a psychoeducational group to develop a set of ground rules is an essential task. In a second-stage group, the ground rules need to be reviewed each time a new member joins the group. Although certain ground rules remain consistent throughout a group's life, others change with the group's developmental stage.

Many survivors will at first be unable to articulate their needs in regards to making the group a safe environment. They are unused to thinking of their needs and unused to having an opportunity to voice them. Negotiating conflicting needs can also be a foreign experience for many survivors. Because of these factors, the ground rules need to be revisited from time to time to ensure that they're still appropriate and timely.

Here are some of the key groundrules that contributors use to make their groups safe environments for their members. It is very important that group leaders use the ground rules to hold the group members accountable to the group process. Violations of the ground rules must be addressed. Many survivors come from families that were chaotic. Having predictable and consistent limits set within the group is an essential step in preparing the ground for the client to take risks and begin to heal.

Confidentiality

Group members are expected to keep information about other group members confidential. They can talk about their own experiences in the group to their friends or to their individual therapist, but they must not identify other group members in their conversations.

Boundaries

Any invasion of another group member's boundaries is unacceptable. Touching can happen only with the agreement of both parties. Sexual relationships between group members are prohibited, at least for the duration of the group. Social relationships outside of the group need to be openly acknowledged so that they do not become a "secret" known to only some group members.

Affective Expression

All feelings are acceptable in the group. However, they cannot be expressed in ways that threaten anyone's safety—either the safety of the survivor who is having the feelings or anyone else's.

Active Participation

Members are expected to be active participants in the group process. Issues between group members are expected to be processed in the group.

Attendance

Group members are expected to attend all group sessions. If a group member is going to be absent from a session, he should notify the group leaders before the meeting. If a client misses more than two consecutive sessions, he has to renegotiate his membership in the group. If a client decides to withdraw from the group, he is asked to announce this to the group and return to the next group session to say "Goodbye."

Pass Rule

Any group member can choose not to participate in any part of the group process, other than the check-in. He is asked to say that he is "choosing to pass" so that the other group members know he is making an active choice and not dissociating or avoiding responsibility.

Sobriety

Group members should not attend the group drunk or stoned, or otherwise unable to engage in the group process.

(Appendix E, "Behaviors That Support Group Process," lists group ground rules developed by one agency to help group members create a positive group environment.)

GROUP PROCESS

Each session should have a predictable opening, middle, and ending stage. Establishing some predictability is a way of making the group into a safe and healing environment.

Most groups begin with a *check-in*, where every group member takes some time to speak to the rest of the group. The focus of this time can be to let the group know how he has been doing since the last session or to identify issues he wants to address in the current session. Some facilitators start groups with questions such as, "What small signs of healing are you noticing in yourself?" or "What part of your body do you like the best and why?" and ask every group member to give his answer as part of his check-in. The questions change every session.

However the check-in is conducted, it needs to be predictable. It also needs to have clear time and content boundaries so that members do not use the check-in to start to do therapy-focused work. Runaway check-ins that become the focus of an entire session reinforce dysfunctional crisis-focused behavior. Even when a client is in crisis, he needs to be supported and contained through the check-in so that everyone has the opportunity to address the group before any one member takes the floor.

The middle section of the session will vary depending on whether it is a first- or second-stage group. In a first-stage group, unless a client has requested time to process an issue, the group will focus on psychoeducational material. Although some affective work may occur, this is not the primary purpose of the group process.

A listing of topics that contributors have used with their first-stage groups includes:

- legal and criminal aspects of sexual abuse
- typical roles in sexually abusive families
- types of offenders
- sex education and information about normal sexual development
- sexual and nonsexual intimacy
- assertiveness
- relationship styles—codependency vs. interdependency
- conflict resolution
- domestic violence—physical, sexual, and emotional abuse
- child development
- parenting skills—consequences vs. punishments
- building self-esteem
- self care and stress-reduction techniques
- self-defeating behaviors

In an eight-to-ten-week group, it would be impossible to address all aspects of abuse-related behavior. The members of the first-stage group should be asked to select the topics that are the most salient to them and these should be the focus of the sessions.

In a second-stage group, the middle stage of the session is unpredictable. This time is used to work with issues that clients identify during the check-in. The exact format this takes will depend upon the style and skills of the group leaders. Whether the focus remains on the individual who raised an issue or whether an issue is worked on by the group as a whole tends to be a function of the group leadership style, the nature of the issue, the level of safety and trust within the group, and the respective ego-strengths of individual group members.

For instance, if a client identifies feelings of shame during check-in, it might be suggested that he work on this individually. This would mean that he would discuss the times when he feels ashamed and he would be offered interventions that would assist him to move through his shame. These interventions may or may not involve the other group members directly. For instance, group members could be asked to act as a mirror for the client and to feed him back both his views of himself and the group members' respective views of him.

Alternatively, all the group members could be enlisted in a shame-focused exercise. They could be asked to write down five of their most shameful experiences on separate pieces of paper. These pieces of paper are placed in an envelope, which is circulated through the group. Each member is asked to pull out one sheet of paper and to read it out aloud. The men's reactions to these anonymous disclosures are then processed. In this procedure, attention is not put on one individual group member; rather, an issue is dealt with by the group as a whole.

Whichever style occurs in the group, after any intense processing it is important that *everyone* have a chance to debrief his experience. Acknowledging the importance of all group members, be they quiet or vocal, close to the end of their healing journey or just starting it, is very important.

In a second-stage group, although the process must be safe, it may not be comfortable. Leehan and Wilson (1985) note that group members form alliances or define their role in the group based on their former family roles. The group leaders will challenge these transferential patterns that clients bring into the group. Clients may be distressed as their habitual ways of interacting with others are challenged and brought into consciousness.

Group leaders need to monitor the types of issues that clients bring into the group and to ensure that there is a reasonable balance of intense process-focused work and enjoyable social interaction. Clients' successes need to be celebrated and shared in equal measure with their pain. The group must concentrate its energies not only on resolving old traumas, but also on building functional new behaviors, such as acknowledging positive events and effective outcomes.

At the close of every session, it is recommended that clients participate in a *ritual closing*. Survivors need time to pull themselves together before they leave the group and return to their regular lives. If the group (or some of its members) has been involved in intense processing, the members need time to debrief this work. Bringing closure to the group process is important. Ritualized questions, such as, "Is there anything you want to say before leaving tonight?" or "What are you going to do for yourself when you get home?" can be part of this closure. After intensive processing, some groups engage in a group hug or some other appropriate activity before closing the session.

Some contributors offer a weekend retreat for their second-stage groups. The group spends a weekend together and stays in a relaxed, comfortable setting. Having a longer time together allows the group members to enter a deeper and more sustained emotional process. Often, as the members speak of their abuse-related histories, new content and feelings emerge.

The longer timeframe permits the group to engage in powerful expressive and symbolic work.

When the time comes for clients to terminate the group process, whether the group is a first- or second-stage group, their departure must be conducted in a thoughtful and appropriate way. Clients need to be well prepared for *termination*. They need plenty of time to replace the support they have received within the group with other nongroup resources. They need to have permission to return to group or other therapeutic processes, should the need arise. Most importantly, however, they need to be aware of the changes they have made by having participated in the group and they need to celebrate their successes. Many clients are reluctant to fully embrace their triumphs because they fear that this will somehow tempt fate. Unintentionally, they discount their own hard-won achievements. The group leaders must address this subtle discounting and support clients in honoring their accomplishments.

GROUP LEADERSHIP

In abuse-focused group therapy, it is important to have two group leaders, especially in a second-stage group. Survivors trigger one another's responses in a group and often more work occurs than one therapist can handle alone. With two therapists in each session, one can take the role of being the primary leader and the other can monitor the less active group members. Quiet clients may, in fact, be quite dissociated and may need support and assistance to return to the here-and-now process of the group.

The two group leaders need to be well matched in their knowledge and skills. Both need to be able to nurture, challenge, and confront clients as the need arises. They need to work together as a team, because group members will often unconsciously try to split them into good therapist and bad therapist, replicating old family patterns.

Both therapists should expect transference reactions from clients from time to time; this may run the gamut from being hated to being adored. Group leaders must ensure that they have adequate time between group sessions to examine these reactions and process their own countertransferential responses. Good supervision is essential to assist the group leaders to separate here-and-now processes from there-and-then transference.

Some contributors argue that the two group leaders should be male, whereas others believe that a male/female co-leadership team is a more appropriate model of group leadership. Both points of view have merit. A male/female team gives the group members opportunities to practice self-disclosure with both sexes and to observe mutually respectful male/female interactions. Indeed, role-modelling a healthy male/female working relationship is often cited as one of the most important benefits of male/female co-leadership. A male/male team challenges group members' beliefs about men. Seeing two male leaders working cooperatively and being either nurturing or confronting as the situation demands challenges clients' preconceived ideas about masculine behavior.

Most contributors agree that the skillfullness of the therapists in working with abuse-related issues is the most important factor. The fact that they work well as a team and are knowledgeable and experienced outweighs considerations of gender. Prior to joining a group, potential members should meet both leaders. If a client is unprepared to work with a male/male team or a mixed gender team, he can be helped to find other treatment resources.

Chapter 9

Critical Issues in Treating Male Survivors

This chapter discusses three critical therapeutic issues. Strategies that contributors have developed to engage male survivors in treatment are presented. Some typical therapeutic impasses that the contributors have encountered are discussed. Finally, opinions about the complex issue of the respective gender of the client and the therapist are examined.

Contributors identified several common themes that recur in their work with male survivors. Many potential clients don't seek therapeutic help because they minimize the impact of having been abused on their adult lives. When male survivors turn to professional services for assistance, they often expect a "quick fix" for their problems and are unprepared for the lengthy self-examination that is an inherent part of abuse recovery.

Negative transference onto authority figures or onto all adults the same sex as the abuser can also contaminate the therapeutic process. Until these dynamics are consciously examined, clients may refuse to engage in treatment because they generalize previous negative experiences to many situations, including therapy.

ENGAGEMENT STRATEGIES

Engaging male sexual abuse survivors in therapy can be difficult. In fact, some contributors said that this is often the hardest therapeutic task.

Since many men don't think of their childhood sexual experience as abusive, they experience cognitive dissonance when a therapist uses sexual abuse terminology in response to their stories. If the client has made no connection between his sexual abuse and his current problems, abuse-focused language seems incongruent to him. If you suspect a client is an abuse survivor, but he is not ready to identify his experience as "abuse" or himself as a "victim," you should use the more generic term "childhood trauma" when referring to the client's past.

Educating male survivors about the ways in which their vulnerable feelings (such as pain, sadness, loss, and abandonment) are disallowed because of cultural factors, while encouraging them to fully experience their lives, gives them permission to redefine their understanding of masculinity.

Personal change and being willing to face one's wounds takes courage and conviction. These qualities fit with traditional models of masculinity; affirming them in the client can make the engagement process proceed more smoothly.

For obvious reasons, survivors have problems trusting others. Clients need to be told that trust is not a prerequisite for recovery—in fact it is more likely an outcome of recovery. The ability to discern who is trustworthy and who isn't and to withhold trust until it is earned should develop during the course of therapy. Safety, however, is a prerequisite for successful therapy. Clear agreements between therapist and their clients are essential; and clients need to have ongoing support to explicitly state their needs regarding safety-related issues. Because these needs are likely to change many times during the course of therapy, clients need to know that safety-focused issues are always open for discussion.

Encouraging clients to adopt a consumer attitude towards therapy gives them permission to choose the person with whom they will work. You can reassure potential clients by suggesting that they interview several clinicians before they make a final choice about which one to engage. During childhood abuse, victims experienced only one option—namely, to go along with the offender. In therapy, clients need to know that they have many options about whom they work with, for what purpose, and for how long.

Therapists should be prepared to be asked, "Are you a survivor yourself?" "What is your sexual orientation?" and "Why do you do this work?" In many forms of therapy, clinicians are expected to respond to such questions by deflecting them back to the client. Although this kind of response certainly has its place in therapy with male survivors, I suggest that before refocusing on the client, clinicians give simple, direct, and honest answers to these questions. Survivors are likely to test your sincerity; ordinarily, you can enhance engagement process by straightforward answers to direct questions.

Predicting certain possible therapeutic occurrences, such as periods of stagnation or actual setbacks, helps clients to accept these events when they occur. If you tell clients in advance that they have a variety of ego states, some of which will operate at an age or stage that doesn't match their chronological age, it gives clients permission to let these repressed parts-of-self to emerge. Clients may regress during flashbacks or hypnotic interventions; normalizing and predicting these kinds of incidents makes them less frightening if and when they occur.

Most survivors need to understand the here-and-now benefits they can expect from therapy. Clients come into therapy expecting progress and relief. They are not prepared for the intense, seemingly negative affects that emerge during abuse-related therapy. Spelling out the present and future benefits of doing therapy can help clients "hang-in" when they're feeling discouraged.

Some clients have little experience with therapy and think that it's like going to see the doctor. They expect a "quick fix" with little or no effort on their part. Educating clients about the therapeutic process and inviting them to weigh its costs and benefits are crucial steps in the early phases of therapy.

Part of educating clients is giving them reasonable estimates of the timeframe they can anticipate for therapy. Although most abuse-related therapy requires at least a year's commitment, the therapeutic process can start with a short contract of four to six sessions. This allows a client to gauge the usefulness of the process and develop some familiarity with it before he makes a decision about committing his time and money to therapy. Offering time-limited and issue-focused contracts can greatly reduce clients' concerns about being overwhelmed by the therapeutic process.

Working with clients to pace and plan the therapy in conjunction with their internal and external resources is a very important part of this work. They need to have sufficient personal resources (e.g., time, money, social support) to engage in the therapeutic process. If therapy becomes a further drain on a survivor's limited resources, he may have to terminate the therapy prematurely, possibly during the Survivor Phase when he is actually more vulnerable than he was prior to entering therapy.

When beginning therapy with male survivors, clinicians must find each client's most comfortable form of processing information and join with it. If a client is very concrete in his orientation, the clinician will also need to be concrete. Frequently this means that therapy with male survivors begins cognitively.

Initially, some survivors are very fearful and don't know what to expect from the therapeutic process. To assist these clients to engage in therapy, clinicians have a responsibility to model willingness and comfort when talking about difficult issues and to provide normalizing information to the client.

Other clients will come into therapy with their emotions worn "on their sleeve." During initial sessions, these clients will need assistance in containing their feelings until they have a more secure relationship with the therapist and can process their vulnerability more safely.

When one is taking a client's abuse-related history, it's very important to give each client permission to pace his disclosure process. If he does not feel safe talking about his abuse experiences, he will probably become dissociative or evasive, which is countertherapeutic. Disclosure about the explicit events that constituted the abuse is generally an ongoing process rather than a one-time event. The parts of the abuse in which the client was active or where he felt the greatest shame are generally the last to be disclosed.

In *Resolving Sexual Abuse*, Dolan (1991) talks about her style of history-taking with abused clients:

> The therapist must communicate a state of concerned attentiveness that is neither voyeuristic in its attention to detail nor minimizing or inadvertently dismissive through lack of sufficient exploration of the actual facts of the victimization. I like to begin by gently asking my client to 'please tell me everything that you feel I need to know in order for you to know that I understand. (p. 26)

This type of respectful inquiry will reassure the client that the therapist has his best interests at heart when asking about anxiety-provoking material. Permission from the therapist to "Tell me as much as you need to for me to understand what happened to you" empowers the client to make decisions about what information to disclose.

Men in recovery are advised not to change their personal relationships until they have reached the Thriver Phase unless the relationship is abusive. Usually, relationships are enhanced by the process of recovery as the client's self-esteem and interpersonal skills undergo positive change.

It's wise to tell clients that they don't have to be better before they start to enjoy life. Enjoying life should be an ongoing process, not a future goal. Taking part in life-enhancing activities that are not focused on recovery assists clients to maintain a balance in their lives.

THERAPEUTIC IMPASSES

Despite clinicians' best efforts to engage their clients in the therapeutic process, there are still occasions when clients reject therapy or terminate prematurely. Certain themes emerged when the contributors were asked to identify the circumstances in which clients are most likely to leave therapy in an untimely fashion.

Experienced clinicians know that for many survivors, subjective life experience worsens during the course of therapy, as memories and feelings that were previous dissociated are reclaimed.

A client has no way of knowing that once he has let go of his maladaptive coping strategies and developed functional coping skills he will find life much more fulfilling. Instead, in the short run, he may perceive therapy as making his life worse rather than better. Consequently many clients prematurely drop out of therapy during the Survivor Phase.

Predicting this experience can help a client to have faith in his own healing and to continue with therapy. Using the metaphor of a trapeze artist can be helpful. A trapeze artist has to let go of one trapeze before he can catch the next one. For a period of time he is hanging in the air without the support of either trapeze; he has to have faith in the momentum that he has built up to carry him successfully to his destination. The therapist may extend the metaphor by pointing out that he or she acts as a safety net throughout the process.

Some survivors have unrealistic expectations about therapy. They enter the therapeutic process believing that it will compensate for all their previous losses and hurts. When the process is unable to meet these expectations, they terminate therapy.

Some survivors have unrealistic expectations about the time it takes to make emotional changes. They want an instant cure for depression, for example, and give up in despair when this does not materialize. They may develop an angry transference to the therapist who is not "fixing" them. The therapist needs to be adept in identifying such a transference and relating it back to its traumatic roots.

Other survivors confuse crisis resolution with recovery and healing. Having entered therapy because of problematic life events, such as a relationship breakdown or problems with authority figures at work, they leave therapy as soon as the immediate crisis associated with this problem is over. They don't realize that although the immediate symptoms may have disappeared, the underlying dynamics are unchanged. Believing that symptom relief is equated with a cure leads many clients to leave therapy prematurely. However, if the problems recur, which they typically do, some clients become more willing to explore the issues that lie at the foundation of their behavior. Hence, it is advisable for therapists to present an early and clear invitation—free of judgement—to their clients to return to therapy at any time.

There is a symmetry between the injunctions (orders received as a child) that a victim received during the abuse and his adult functioning. When a client is not prepared to confront and change an injunction, his loyalty to this injunction can result in his leaving therapy. For instance, if a victim was told by his abuser that his life would be in danger if he ever talked about the abuse, it's possible that talking about the abuse in therapy may create too much anxiety for him to be able to continue.

For clients who were severely and/or ritualistically abused, prohibitive injunctions can lessen their abilities to process abuse-related material. Engaging MPD clients whose "persecutor alters" remain loyal to the abuser(s) can be a complex and sensitive task. For clients who were less severely sexually abused, you need to identify injunctions in terms of both their content and the person who issued them. Cognitive reality testing and empowering expressive work that challenges the old injunction is generally effective in reducing its power.

Certain survivors have developed secondary gains from their victim-based identities, and they may resist therapy because they want to avoid changing dysfunctional life patterns. If they do not see the benefits of changing, and can see only the accompanying anxiety and effort, they will not invest in the therapeutic process. Often, such survivors have inadequate social or work-related skills; before they can anticipate making substantive changes in their lives, they first have to acquire skills that will support such changes. For example, if a victim has projected his anger at his abuser onto his bosses and has continually lost jobs by getting into power struggles with his employers, he may need to develop anger control and conflict resolution skills before he can stabilize his life sufficiently to begin abuse-focused therapy.

THERAPIST GENDER ISSUES

Clients who have been abused will unconsciously project their past experience onto the present; in many cases, their relationship with the abuser, or some aspects of it, will be projected onto the therapist. These projections, or transferences, need to be decoded and understood in order for the client to become aware of his unconscious patterns. The therapist's gender, as well as the therapist's personal behavior or characteristics, can be responsible for eliciting transferential projections. Gender-focused transference will have unique aspects for each client, depending on his perpetrator's gender, his own sexual orientation, and idiosyncratic aspects of the abuse experience.

There is some debate in the treatment community about the importance of the gender of the therapist who treats male survivors. Some say that men who have been abused by a male must be treated by other men in order to restore a healthy sense of masculinity; others, and I am one, believe that the gender of the therapist is a relatively minor issue compared to his or her competence.

Therapists who believe male survivors are best served by male clinicians put forward arguments based in social learning theory and gender politics. They believe that men who have been injured by other men need to heal from these injuries by receiving nurturance and skillful assistance from a male clinician. An implicit message of male support is present when a male client works with a male therapist, and the male therapist is a role model for appropriate, nonabusive male caring. A male clinician has a similar set of cultural gender experiences to inform his work with male clients, and this makes him a more appropriate helping agent than a female clinician. When a male client works through his issues about his sexual vulnerability or his discomfort with his gender identity with a male clinician, these issues can, according to this position, be more deeply resolved than they would be if the therapist were female. (Female clinicians who work with female survivors have used almost identical arguments to support a female client/female therapist model of treatment.)

In some cases, practical rather than theoretical reasons are given to support the position that male clients are better served by male therapists. Since many males, including male survivors, have internalized misogynist, or sexist, cultural beliefs, it is proposed that men enter the therapeutic process more easily when they can engage with another man. According to these views, a woman therapist will not have the same credibility in the client's eyes, and clients will either dismiss the therapy process as "feminine" or attempt to turn it into a social event. Some suggest that adolescent clients are too embarrassed to discuss their sexuality or sexual abuse with a female therapist and that such clients are better served by male clinicians.

Clinicians who believe that the therapist's gender is an irrelevant or minor variable in the healing process tend to use humanist arguments to endorse their practices. Their position is based on the belief that the safety, respect, empathy, integrity, openness, competence, and experience that a therapist brings to his or her work are more important than his or her gender. For these clinicians, everything a client presents is grist for the mill of therapy. When a client's transference is elicited by a clinician, male or female, the transference provides good therapeutic material to work with.

In group therapy, members of this school of thought use a mixed gender leadership team because they believe that such a team has the added benefit of modelling appropriate male/female relationship and that both leaders can provide nurturing, respectful support irrespective of their gender.

There is a range of opinion about the importance of the respective genders of the therapist and the client amongst the contributors to this study. Some firmly believe that although the therapeutic process may initially be slower, a survivor who was abused by a male will ultimately be better served if therapy is provided by a male clinician. Others are adamant that gender issues are political rather than therapeutic; their overriding concern is that clients receive good therapy.

All theoretical considerations aside, decisions about which clients receive therapy from which clinicians often reflect administrative rather than therapeutic concerns. A client's financial circumstances may limit his therapeutic choices. Some agencies process clients on a "first come, first served" basis, and decisions about client/therapist fit are accordingly compromised. In other agencies, the only staff who are knowledgeable about sexual abuse issues are female and, for better or worse, these are the clinicians who serve male survivors.

Ideally, each client should have free choice about the gender of his therapist. Clients' fears, conscious or unconscious, about revictimization and their sense of whom they feel safe with are very idiosyncratic. Both client and therapist need to trust the client's intuition about which gender initially feels the most comfortable, because therapy needs to begin with the greatest possible sense of safety.

Eventually, survivors need to embrace both genders; at some time in the recovery process, they will probably find it helpful to work with their less preferred gender. The only rule that must be followed is that clients must never be forced to work with a clinician they don't feel safe with, be this gender-based or otherwise, because this replicates the original abuse dynamic.

Gender fit between a client and a therapist should ideally be based on the client's needs. In a similar fashion, a client's sexual orientation and ethnicity are other variables that must be considered when selecting a therapist. The gay subculture has unique norms governing sexuality and relationships. Given the heterosexist nature of our culture, many therapists are unfamiliar with the mores and nuances of gay subculture. Therapists who are working with gay clients must be willing to examine their own heterosexist attitudes and assumptions and to learn about their clients' subculture. Ethnic diversities also need to be discussed in the process of choosing a therapist; again, the client's choice of therapist ethnicity must be honored in order for him to reestablish his personal power.

Chapter 10

Counselling Adolescent Male Survivors

This chapter focuses on therapy for adolescent male survivors of sexual abuse. Difficulties with engaging this population in treatment are discussed, and some means of increasing the likelihood of therapeutic engagement are provided. Issues regarding assessment process with adolescents, including assessing their motivational level and their maturity, are discussed. Guidelines for working with this population are presented and several interventions that contributors have developed to work with this population are outlined. Finally, group treatment is recommended as a treatment modality of choice for this population because of its developmental appropriateness.

Adolescent victims of sexual abuse are no different from adult survivors in the ways they are affected. Both feel betrayal, stigmatization, shame, and anger. Both have questions about masculinity and sexual identity. Developmentally, however, adolescent victims are different from adults, and their therapy must reflect these differences.

Adolescents are still forming their physical, psychological, and sexual identities. They have more changeable personas than adults, and are more willing to experiment with a variety of different, and often contrary, psychosocial styles. Adolescents are very influenced by their peers. For most teenagers, being accepted by their peer culture is paramount; the parts of self that they most consciously identify with generally reflect the values of their current peer group.

Adolescent males who have been sexually abused are reluctant to incorporate experiences they consider deviant (such as their sexual abuse) into their sexual personas. Adolescent boys tend to accept the myth that says they are expected to know all about sexual matters, no matter what the limits of their personal knowledge. Admitting they have concerns about sexuality is considered "uncool."

For many adolescent victims, the power of culturally approved mythologies about sexuality and masculinity overwhelms their own experience. Because of this, many of them deny their victimization. They either repress their memories of having been abused or rewrite their histories and describe the abuse as consensual. Since many offenders are skillful at giving responsibility for their actions to their victims, this misconstruction of reality is generally also supported by the perpetrator. Other victims clearly see their abuse as exploitive, but deny its having had any impact on them (Froning & Mayman, 1990).

Ironically, it is often easier for adolescent victims to discuss their sexual offenses against others than it is to discuss their own victimization because offending behaviors conform better to cultural expectations about masculine power and control. Many adolescent victims who participate in counselling first enter treatment facilities as adolescent sexual offenders. Adolescent victims who do not act out their abuse-reactive behaviors in ways that cause concern to others are frequently never treated, especially if their discomfort with their victimization keeps them silent.

Adolescents tend to think of themselves as invincible. They are not usually aware of the circumstances and/or needs of their childhood that left them vulnerable to being abused. They blame themselves for their victimization. Still forming their identities, they don't see their relationship difficulties or dysfunctional behaviors as being related to sexual victimization. They don't have an extensive history of intimacy problems to motivate them to examine the origin of these difficulties. Instead, they tend to see themselves as secretly flawed or they accept their difficulties as inevitable, characterological traits.

THE ROLE OF COUNSELLING WITH
ADOLESCENT MALE VICTIMS

Therapy is a countercultural experience for adolescent males. Male self-reliance, independence, and action-based behaviors are challenged by the therapeutic process. For many adolescent victims, participating in therapy has connotations of "being crazy" or "sick." It's a challenge for clinicians to package therapy so that it can be a helpful and nonstigmatizing experience for adolescent victims.

Whether his sexual abuse was intrafamilial or extrafamilial will have an impact on an adolescent victim's therapeutic experience. In either circumstance, the victim's family needs to be involved in treatment if he is living at home. If the abuse was intrafamilial, other family members will also need to be involved in extensive counselling processes. If the family members want to remain together, their treatment will involve intensive individual, group, and family therapy. Even when families have responded appropriately to the disclosure of abuse, the adolescent male victim's recovery will be enhanced by family therapy.

For adolescent clients who live independently from their families, family therapy may be impossible. Adolescents in foster or residential care, or those living on their own, need support within their immediate community if they are going to address their victimization. If this support does not exist or if there are other more pressing issues that are preoccupying the adolescent, focusing on abuse-related events is counter-therapeutic. Waiting until an adolescent is ready to address his victimization is a very important aspect of the therapeutic process.

An adolescent needs the support and caring of his family and community to fully integrate and resolve his victimization. The victim's family (or community) also needs assistance. If inadequate parental supervision contributed to the boy's victimization, the clinician must address this, especially if there are young children in the family. Other families overprotect children who have been victimized; they excuse all aberrant behavior, no matter what its origin, because of the abuse.

Counselling adolescent male survivors of sexual abuse takes a different focus from that taken with adults. Counselling is the operative word, rather than therapy, since the process concentrates on skill building rather than on trauma resolution. This does not mean that trauma resolution does not occur. It does. However, with adolescent clients, abreactive-type processes are not invoked in the same way as with adult survivors. Very few adolescent victims have a sufficiently mature personality or sufficiently well-developed ego strengths to undertake voluntary abreactive processing. However, in their favor, adolescent victims have rarely built up the same entrenched dissociative processes that cause abreactions and hence they can often process their abuse-related experiences more directly.

Adolescent clients need to deal with the impacts of having been abused that are currently affecting their lives. Often this means that treatment focuses on issues such as sexual expression and sexual identity. They need to be helped to see that sexuality is, in itself, a positive force in their lives, but that nonconsensual sex is damaging. They need to be helped to distinguish between peer contacts and power contacts in regard to sex. Their understanding of sexuality needs to be expanded to include more than genital sexual arousal.

Clinicians also need to prepare adolescents for the possibility that they may need to revisit their sexual abuse and its impact on their lives as they pass through different developmental stages. This possibility must be handled with a light touch to ensure that it doesn't become a self-fulfilling prophecy. However, it is common for sexual abuse victims to examine their abuse-related experiences as they mature. For instance, when an abuse victim becomes a father and fully understands the vulnerability of children in the face of adult power, his grief for his own lost childhood may be reactivated. Hence, counselling needs to be a positive experience for adolescent clients—to keep the door open for future therapy, should the need arise.

ASSESSING ADOLESCENT VICTIMS OF SEXUAL ABUSE

Most adolescent males are not used to talking explicitly with adults about their sexuality. In fact, if this has happened at all, it has generally occurred within the context of being sexually abused. Hence, an assessing clinician must make his or her role and intent very clear to abused clients, so that they don't think that the assessment is an elaborate new grooming procedure.

If assessments are to provide useful diagnostic information, clients must cooperate by giving truthful and detailed answers to the questions asked. In order for this to happen, the client must be confident that the assessment process will help him.

Some adolescents respond to an invitation to "lift the burden of secrecy" that has surrounded their abuse. If they see talking about their abuse as a means of relieving their feelings of stigmatization and low self-esteem, they will cooperate more easily with the assessment process.

Explaining the assessment procedure and the assessor's role to adolescent clients is an essential first step in establishing a trusting relationship. This is especially important if the assessor will not be the client's ongoing therapist. Clients need to know in advance if they will be assessed by one clinician, but treated by another.

Using a medical analogy can help adolescent victims understand why they have to reveal intimate information about their abuse. The assessing clinician can tell the client that if someone experiencing severe stomach cramps were taken to an emergency ward, the doctor who examined him would need to know why he was having so much pain before treating him; otherwise, the patient might be subjected to surgery when in reality he only needed to get rid of some stomach gas. In the same way, an assessment enables the clinician to be skillful in his interventions. The information that he receives from the client assists him to formulate an effective treatment plan.

During a good assessment, the clinician will educate the client about both abuse and treatment processes. Since adolescent male victims often feel a great deal of shame about having repeatedly been involved in abuse, they need to be reassured about the normalcy of their behavior. If an assessing clinician tells the client that abuse victims usually have very good reasons for *not* telling anyone about the abuse, and then asks the client if he had reasons for not telling, this eases the client's shame for not having told when the abuse began.

Adolescent clients also carry shame about their physical arousal during the abuse. Sharing basic physiological information can assist the assessment process. When an adolescent client understands that if his penis is stimulated it will become erect, no matter who is stimulating it or why, he feels less ashamed discussing his arousal. In a humorous way, the assessing clinician can remind an adolescent client that his penis doesn't have eyes or a brain or any other way to determine who is stimulating it.

The clinician needs to show adolescents that when an event happens it can be understood in many different ways. Clients may have interpreted their physiological response to the abuse by thinking "I'm very sexy" or "I'm gay" or "I'm a pervert"; these interpretations may have limited their understanding of the abuse. Helping clients to see how they made sense of being victimized can give them permission to become less self blaming in their interpretation of these events. This can increase their ease in discussing abuse-related matters. Often, a simple analogy can help clients see how interpretation changes our understanding of an event. For example, if you have been expecting a telephone call from a friend who doesn't call, you'll react differently if you think your friend has had an accident from the way you'll act if you think your friend is mad at you.

Adolescent clients need to know that their strengths as well as their weaknesses are important to the assessing clinician. The assessment process should focus on gathering information in as much detail as possible. This includes information about the client's successes and positive coping skills.

If a client displays cognitive errors, such as being very self-blaming, these need to be noted, but not challenged, during the assessment. The treatment stage of therapy is the time to change thinking errors, not the assessment stage (Gerber, 1990a). If the assessor prematurely challenges dysfunctional cognitive patterns, the client may feel unheard or misunderstood, and may subsequently withdraw from disclosing any further personal information.

Frequently, everyone in an adolescent's life, except the adolescent himself, wants him to get treatment. If an adolescent is not motivated to address his abuse-related issues, treatment will only reinforce his experience of dysfunctional power dynamics. An adolescent client needs to know that he is a partner in the treatment process and that he is in charge of what he will tell the clinician about himself and when he will do so.

Forcing an adolescent into treatment before he is motivated is countertherapeutic. The only exception to this rule occurs when an adolescent is abusing younger children and must be held accountable so that he doesn't continue to endanger others.

During the assessment process, an adolescent client's ego strengths and ability to handle anxiety must be determined. If focusing on his sexual abuse will increase his destructive behavior towards himself or others, it is not advisable to proceed. Many adolescents do not have sufficiently sophisticated coping strategies to contain the emotions that surface when they recall their abuse. If this is the case, their treatment must focus on building self-care skills, rather than on abuse-related material per se.

An adolescent client's dissociative tendencies need to be assessed prior to treatment. Dissociative adolescents are often self-destructive, experience drastic mood swings, and act out behaviorally in ways that are inconsistent with their primary personas. (A test to assess adolescent dissociation called the Dean Adolescent Inventory Scale is included in Appendix F, page 185.)

(For more detailed information about assessment issues for adolescent male victims of sexual abuse, including specific assessment questions, see "The Assessment Interview for Young Male Victims" by Paul Gerber. A reference for this article can be found in References.)

THE TREATMENT PROCESS WITH
ADOLESCENT VICTIMS OF SEXUAL ABUSE

Adolescent victims of sexual abuse exhibit the same wide range of symptoms and strengths as their adult counterparts. However, due to their youth, adolescents have had less opportunity to internalize dysfunctional coping mechanisms. They are at a developmental stage that encourages experimentation, and are often more willing than adults to try out new behaviors provided they don't feel embarrassed or humiliated doing so.

Therapist's Style

Therapists who work with adolescents must be comfortable with this age group. They need to be able to work with erratic mood swings and attitudinal challenges without becoming parental. The therapist needs to be confident in his or her own role, but not authoritarian. The therapist must be comfortable with adolescent clients' jargon and language. Adolescent communication styles and sexual nomenclature come in and out of fashion; the therapist needs to keep abreast of these trends.

Gender of Therapist

Adolescent male victims are generally more at ease discussing their sexuality with a male therapist. Knowing that the therapist has a similar psychophysiological reality from which to discuss sexuality enhances the client's level of comfort. However, if an adolescent client was abused by a male, discussing the abuse with a female therapist may initially feel safer. It is important that clients' preferences about the gender of their therapist be respected and honored.

Clear Boundaries and Limits

Therapists must explicitly state that during the course of counselling adolescent clients will be expected to talk about their sexuality, but that they will always be in charge of how much, or how little, they say. Therapists who work with adolescent survivors need to approach sexuality with a "no big deal" attitude and convey a direct and relaxed approach to sexual issues.

Typically, adolescent clients will test their therapists' abilities to handle sexual material. The therapists' responses will determine the extent to which the client engages in the therapeutic process. Therapists can assume that a client won't disclose the full extent of his abuse until he feels confident that he is safe to do so. Asking questions such as, "What else happened?" or "Is there something more to tell me about what happened to you?" can help the client make a full disclosure. Asking, "What kind of sexual experiences have you had?" is a nonstigmatizing way to ask about abuse and will generally elicit more information than questions that contain the words "sexual abuse."

Not only must the therapist be explicit regarding his or her expectations that the client's sexuality will be discussed during his counselling, but he or she must also be explicit in regards to other therapeutic boundaries and limits.

Adolescent clients need to know the therapist's boundary of confidentiality. Therapists must state that they will break therapeutic confidentiality if they're concerned about the safety of the client or of anyone else. For instance, if the client discloses information about other abusive incidents, the therapist is legally bound to report them. If other members of the client's family are also in treatment, the client needs to know how information will be shared between the different treatment providers. You also need to clarify whether your client will be given information from other family members' sessions, and vice versa.

Counselling Process

Treatment with adolescent victims generally proceeds best if it is short-term. It needs to clearly focus on the presenting problem or issue that is most pertinent to the client. Partializing treatment so that it deals with one piece of work at a time is a good strategy to use with adolescent survivors. Creating a succession of small successes boosts clients' self-esteem. It also ensures that the treatment process is a positive experience for the client, thus increasing the likelihood that he will use therapeutic resources in the future.

For example, if an adolescent victim is acting out by being aggressive with authority figures (unconsciously displacing his anger at his abuser onto other adult figures), his therapeutic contract might focus on anger expression and developing safe and effective ways to manage his angry feelings. The therapist might make some attempt to connect his present anger with his past betrayal, but the primary focus of therapy would be on assisting the client to address his here-and-now concerns. Once he had learned and integrated these new skills, the contract would end. The therapist would encourage the client to renew therapy if in the future he developed new psychosocial problems or showed other symptoms related to his sexual abuse.

Adolescents often engage more quickly with the therapeutic process if they can approach abuse-specific issues with a little distance. This can occur in a variety of ways. One method is to use externalizing techniques, such as drawing or other art media.

Asking an adolescent male survivor to draw what he would like to do to his perpetrator can be a stimulus to discussing anger and a constructive means of channelling intense feelings. Often boys have chosen dangerous or socially unacceptable ways to express their anger (such as putting a fist through a window), and they need to find safe ways to discharge this emotion. Some boys are so afraid of the power of their rage that they have shut down their angry responses, and their anger is sublimated into other areas of their life. For clients like these, it is very beneficial to develop assertiveness skills and to learn to separate anger and violence.

Psychoeducational materials help adolescent clients process their abuse. They not only fill in information deficits that the clients may have, but also act as door openers for more personal disclosures. For example, if a client is reluctant to share any information about the specifics of his abuse, you can give him a set of flash cards that have different types of touching described on them. (The cards can include behaviors such as hugging, kissing on the cheek, French kissing, touching someone's breasts, shaking hands, fellatio, punching someone, etc.). Ask the client to sort the cards into three piles: OK touch, not-OK touch, and unclear touch. His choices and his reasons for making these choices can then be discussed. You can ask more participatory clients to generate their own list of different types of touch.

Sometimes, reading adolescents stories that were originally intended for younger children can stimulate discussion about events in their childhood. The client's developmental age is often younger than his chronological age. Provided that he doesn't experience being read to as condescending, his inner child will often be activated by more juvenile reading material. This kind of stimulation can "unfreeze" parts of the self that had shut down at the time of the sexual abuse. In a similar manner, showing videos and movies that deal with abuse can be an indirect way of accessing abuse-related material. (See Resources for a listing of video and written resources.)

Separating the parts of self that a client accepts from those that he rejects or is uncomfortable with can be a first step in working towards integration. It may help to refer to the different parts of the clients as "sad Bob," "angry Bob," or "scared Bob" and talk about them as if they were separate.

To reshape a client's sexual behavior into more age-appropriate forms, it's often necessary to work with the client's sexual fantasies. The use of guided imagery can be helpful in this regard. For example, after bringing your client into deep relaxation, ask him to imagine a place of safety for himself that is the most beautiful place that he knows. Tell him that he will have complete privacy in this place and ask him to think about what he'd like to do sexually that would give him the biggest possible turn-on. Ask him if it involves anyone else. If he says "Yes," ask him to note the person's name. (Be careful not to specify an age or gender in order to give the client room to fully develop his own fantasy.) Ask your client to thank the person for joining him in his fantasy and to let the person leave the fantasy in the smoothest possible way. (Actually imagining the sexual behavior with the other person is discouraged because this only reinforces possibly deviant behavior.) Then you gradually bring the client back into the counselling session. The fantasy and the role of the person or persons the client called into his fantasy are debriefed. If the client's arousal patterns are based on deviant behaviors, he is helped to develop more orthodox associations to sexual stimulation.

Adolescent clients need help to develop safety plans to reduce the possibility of being revictimized, or protective steps to follow should they actually become revictimized. This is especially important for clients who were intrafamilially abused and who continue to live at home. In such cases, all the family members need to be involved in developing "fire drills" to put into effect should any member of the family have concerns about either their own or another family member's safety. These "fire drills" can consist of ensuring that all family members, especially the victim, have a trusted person to whom they can turn if they have safety concerns. In some cases, they involve family contracts about how certain family members agree to interact with one another. Whatever form they take, they're essential to ensure that adolescent clients are familiar with both preventative and crisis-based self-care strategies.

Group Treatment

Group treatment is a particularly effective treatment modality for adolescent victims of sexual abuse. Given that adolescents are peer-focused and many have negative associations with one-to-one contact with an adult because of their victimization, group treatment is a safe and effective form of treatment. The group process breaks the adolescent victim's isolation and helps him to destigmatize his victimization. Peer contact with other victims encourages adolescent survivors to openly acknowledge their abuse experience.

A group format gives clients options about how much or how little of themselves they disclose, since they are no longer the single focus of a therapist's attention. For many adolescent victims, being able to move in and out of the spotlight makes the group process more comfortable than individual counselling sessions, where they are always the center of attention. The control this gives adolescent clients generally increases their feelings of safety and hence they participate more freely in the treatment process.

It is recommended that therapists provide the same two-stage group treatment model to their adolescent clients that was described for adult survivors in Chapter 8. Although the discussion in an adolescent group will reflect the developmental concerns of this population, the therapeutic issues regarding assessment and group processes are the same as for an adult group.

Chapter 11

Therapist Issues

Because therapy is an interactive process, the well-being and integrity of the therapist has a fundamental impact on the course of therapy for the client. Clients will intuitively be aware of inconsistencies between what a therapist says and what he or she does. This section of the text describes important self-care strategies for therapists to incorporate into their work and lives. It suggests seven ways to recognize and manage therapists' countertransference. Finally, I briefly mention some special concerns for therapists who are themselves survivors of childhood sexual abuse.

Providing therapy to male survivors has many intrinsic rewards. The intimacy of the therapeutic process and the chance to participate in a client's healing and growth provide a therapist with both professional and personal satisfaction. A therapist's confidence and effectiveness build as he or she develops specialized skills for working with survivors and as his or her intuition in applying these skills becomes more finely tuned.

However, empathetic listening to survivors' experiences leaves the therapist open to experience of vicarious trauma and loss. Ironically, Briere (1989) suggests that the therapeutic empathy of clinicians makes them especially vulnerable to personally incorporating the trauma expressed by their clients, thereby creating a secondary victim in the therapist.

The phenomenon of vicarious traumatization, or traumatization by proxy, is one that all therapists who work extensively with clients who have experienced childhood trauma must learn to manage. Finding the balance between being able to absorb and respond therapeutically to the events that clients disclose and distancing themselves from this information as a means of self-protection is an ongoing issue for therapists.

Not only do therapists vicariously experience their clients' trauma, but they may be directly affected if a client's story triggers unresolved issues from the therapist's past history. Some therapists report violent and disturbing dreams after working with survivors (Briere, 1989). Clinicians who work with abuse survivors need to have ongoing supervision to help them process their responses to their clients; in some cases, personal therapy is an important component of therapist self-care.

Therapists who work with clients who have been sexually abused often become more vigilant about their own or their children's personal safety. Several contributors commented that after working with many survivors of sexual abuse they view the world more cynically and less trustingly than before. There are certainly some personal costs for the therapist who works extensively with abuse survivors.

Because therapy is an interactive process between two people, each is subject to being influenced by the other. Given the nature of the therapeutic contract, it is essential for therapists to develop strategies to handle their own countertransference so as not to act it out in therapy. In addition, therapists must become aware of their own thematic life issues so that they don't unconsciously play them out with clients.

Here are some countertransferential concerns that therapists commonly experience and procedures to reduce their negative impact on both client and therapist.

COUNTERTRANSFERENCE IN THERAPY
WITH MALE SURVIVORS

Therapists, as well as clients, internalize cultural attitudes and gender scripts. To the extent that the therapists are unconsciously acting out such scripts and attitudes, they may unknowingly project them onto their client relationships. Such contamination of the therapeutic process needs to be identified, challenged, and transformed. Just as therapists support their clients in challenging ways of living that are no longer useful, so they themselves need to be challenged and supported in developing and enhancing their therapeutic skills.

The emotions and dysfunctional behaviors that male survivors present can elicit a range of responses in the therapist. It is not unusual for therapists to begin to develop the same kinds of defenses shown by their clients during their work together. Therapist dissociation, minimization, avoidance, helplessness, and other similar parallel processes can occur.

Generally, a change in the therapist's affective state or behavior indicates the presence of countertransferential dynamics. For example, some therapists start to feel sleepy when their clients discuss material that echoes their own thematic issues. Other therapists will redirect their clients' attention to less emotionally charged material when their own anxiety levels begin to rise. If a therapist starts to dread his sessions with a particular client, or begins to feel overwhelmed and incompetent in the face of a client's issues, he or she is probably experiencing countertransference. Learning to notice these cues and using them as signals for self-examination can reduce the negative impact of these dynamics on the therapy.

Another aspect of countertransference occurs when a therapist begins to see a client as "special" and deserving extra attention. Extending the length of sessions at no extra cost to the client, or meeting with a client outside of scheduled sessions, or in other ways changing the normal boundaries of the therapeutic relationship indicates that the therapist is exhibiting countertransferential dynamics that need to be addressed in the therapist's supervision.

At times, it is necessary to change the normal boundaries of the therapeutic relationship and hold longer sessions or meet more frequently. However, the therapist needs to ensure that these changes are the result of sound clinical judgement, not unconscious countertransference. Whenever a therapist's interaction with a client is driven by his or her own needs, rather than by the client's needs, he or she is opening the possibility of replicating the original abuse dynamics. Being aware of this potential hazard and working to avoid it are important aspects of therapy with survivors.

MANAGING COUNTERTRANSFERENCE

Following are contributors' suggestions for managing countertransference and providing self-care:

- a partnership attitude to providing therapy;
- personal therapy for the therapist;
- identifying one's personal limits and boundaries;
- supervision;

- peer support;
- advocacy; and
- personal life satisfaction.

A Partnership Attitude to Providing Therapy

Therapists who work with male survivors often need to remind them-selves that the power to heal from childhood trauma lies in the client, not in the therapist. Like good gardeners, therapists can nurture and fertilize their clients' growth. They may assist in removing noxious weeds or other hindrances to full recovery. However, the therapists need to trust that their clients, like growing plants, have an inherent ability to respond favorably to appropriate interventions.

Victims of abuse need to be in control of pacing their recovery pro-cess. A therapist who adopts an authoritarian stand with clients will generally elicit countertherapeutic transference. Therapists who see them-selves as facilitators who can guide their clients' recovery, rather than as experts who can prescribe cures, are more likely to help their clients. Not only is sharing power in therapy an essential component of restoring the client's capacity to make autonomous decisions, but letting go of a need to control the process reduces the therapist's work-related stress.

Several contributors commented on the importance of therapists being responsive to their clients and to the issues they present without taking responsibility for them. Clients need to be given complete ownership of their own actions, beliefs, behaviors, and cognitions. The therapist's task is to be able to respond to all aspects of the client nonjudgementally. Therapists must avoid taking a parental stance with clients since this will generally counteract the desired outcome of increasing the client's autonomy.

Therapists express a partnership attitude toward their clients when they own their own shortcomings and imperfections. Inevitably, all therapists make mistakes with their clients. For instance, a therapist may misjudge the timing of an intervention or he may interrupt a client prematurely to give well-intentioned feedback. To the extent that therapists can claim mistakes such as these, they provides their clients with a model for honest human interaction. Therapists' personal integrity and the congruence be-tween their words and deeds influence the success of therapy as much as their professional knowledge and expertise do.

Therapy for the Therapist

There are several important reasons why therapists who work with adult survivors of childhood trauma should have undergone, or be engaged in, psychotherapy. Probably foremost of these is that by coming to terms with their own psychological scripts, therapists are less likely to project their own injuries onto others—most notably their clients. It is important to understand the process of therapeutic change not just intellectually, but also experientially, in order to genuinely engage and track one's clients.

Due to the intense nature of therapy with survivors of childhood sexual trauma, it is likely that therapists will face their own psychological vulnerabilities. Each therapist will have idiosyncratic triggers that particular clients will provoke. For instance, one therapist may typically overwork on behalf of clients who are very depressed, in response to his own family script about how to handle depressed feelings. Another therapist may become angry or afraid when clients identify issues similar to his or her own childhood trauma, thereby unconsciously inhibiting the client's safety to work on these issues.

Personal therapy helps therapists to more easily separate their own processes from those of their clients. Therapists will be better able to identify their own vulnerable areas and to work more effectively with clients who provoke them.

Good personal therapy should assist therapists in developing skills that make them more fully present in both their work and personal lives. It should provide them with skills to respond to their own personal process should a client unknowingly trigger a problematic association. For example, if during a session a therapist's child ego state is evoked by a client, the therapist can hold a brief inner dialogue with his or her own inner child to negotiate how to address the issue after the session. In this way, the therapy session remains client-focused, while the person of the therapist is also respected.

If a therapist in personal therapy is conducting therapy with clients, it is essential that he or she have good clinical supervision to keep personal issues distinct from client issues. Therapists need to be respectful of themselves and to structure their time in self-supporting ways. For instance, personal therapy appointments need to be scheduled at a time when you can be self-focused and do not immediately have to return to client-focused concerns. There may be times when you will have to lighten your workload if you are working intensely on personal issues.

Identifying One's Personal Limits and Boundaries

Therapists who work with survivors of childhood trauma need to create clear and predictable boundaries in their work to support both their clients and themselves. For clients, knowing the therapist's ground rules about issues such as scheduling extra sessions or handling unpaid fees provides safety and predictability. For the therapist, setting up clear boundaries is good self-care.

Therapists must have clear policies about missed appointments, receiving crisis phone calls, extended sessions, fee payments, and so on. When to schedule vacations and the length of a typical work day are decisions that need to be tailored to a therapist's personal taste and style.

Other boundaries are more general in nature and focus on broader issues. Managing case-load composition in ways that respect your own needs is a vital aspect of setting boundaries. When determining what types of clients the therapist will work with and the size of his or her caseload, the therapist must be thoughtful and realistic about his or her circumstances. In general, it is advisable for therapists who work with sexual abuse survivors to maintain a mixed caseload. Clients who are recovering from childhood sexual trauma are usually candidates for long-term therapy. Having opportunities to work with short-term cases and a variety of presenting problems can help to keep the therapist refreshed and energized.

It is important that the boundaries a therapist sets be flexible enough to change to meet new eventualities, but rigid enough to meet the purpose for which they were intended. Ensuring that clients are aware of their therapists' work-related boundaries is a key ingredient of ensuring that therapy remain a safe and predictable process.

Almost inevitably, clients will ask their therapist why they do the work they do. Therapists who choose to work with sexual abuse survivors have a multitude of reasons for doing so. These reasons need to be clear to the therapist; often they emerge during the course of the therapist's own therapy. Although therapists must be judicious about the personal information they tell clients, you should be prepared to honestly answer your clients' inquiries about why you work with sexual abuse survivors.

Sexual abuse, by definition, has involved a violation of a client's personal boundary. In the therapeutic process, therefore, the therapist must be vigilant about respecting his or her clients' boundaries while simultaneously respecting his or her own. Providing both clients and therapists with a safe environment in which to engage in the therapeutic process is paramount and any lapse in maintaining clear boundaries that may jeopardize this safety must be avoided.

Supervision

Regular supervision with a therapist who is knowledgeable about the dynamics of sexual abuse and recovery from this trauma is an essential aspect of therapist self-care. Several contributors noted that no matter how skillful they think they have become in providing therapeutic services to survivors, they continue to schedule regular supervision and consultation sessions on a weekly or a biweekly basis.

Good clinical supervision can serve a variety of functions. It is an opportunity for therapists to share their own responses to their clients' issues and to assess their own needs. A supervisor can also reflect aspects of the therapeutic relationship (such as countertransference and transference) that the therapist is not aware of. Given the emotional intensity of therapy, the therapist's ability to objectively assess each case can be lost. His or her supervisor, who is not directly involved, can maintain the role of an objective observer. A supervisor can help a therapist identify recurrent themes that emerge across several cases. These themes may reflect the therapist's unresolved personal issues or work style rather than his or her clients' clinical needs.

For instance, clients often present with a "let's-get-this-over-with-quickly" attitude. Therapists with their own issues about getting things done quickly may collude with the client's impatience even though it is countertherapeutic to rush into abreactive work before establishing therapeutic rapport and building a client's self-care skills. A skillful supervisor can help a therapist recognize his or her tendency to proceed too quickly, thus assisting both therapist and client in the process. In ways such as this, supervision provides therapists with instruction, ideas, and support for their work.

Peer Support

In addition to the support of formal supervision, both formal and informal peer support enhances a therapist's abilities and enthusiasm. It is not unusual for clinicians to experience isolation in their work, especially if they work privately without team support. Creating opportunities to discuss cases and their personal and professional impact with peers who are engaged in similar work is very rewarding. Many contributors are members of peer support groups that meet regularly and they say these collegial networks are of great value to them.

Some contributors note that although the work they do is serious, it need not be solemn. It's important to find humor, both in the therapeutic process and in interactions with peers. Several contributors remarked that a valued feature of their peer support group is that it provides a safe forum to express humor or make "politically incorrect" statements about their work. Being able to make jokes about therapy in a safe environment helps these therapists to unload work-related stress.

Advocacy

For many therapists, incorporating a preventative or educational component into their work acts as a good counterbalance to their therapeutic work with clients. When therapists focus solely on helping individual clients to recover from childhood sexual trauma, they can lose sight of the social and cultural aspects of this problem. Creating opportunities to work at social change can remind a therapist of the political, ethical, or spiritual reasons that motivated his or her career choice.

Contributors mentioned a variety of ways that they work toward social change. Many are involved in public education; they write articles and books on abuse-related issues or present workshops about abuse to the general public or to other professionals. Others see their work as part of the global struggle for improving human rights and give time and energy to political or humanistic organizations. Regardless of the specific avenue of expression, working within social networks to curtail sexual abuse can boost your sense of purpose and reaffirm the importance of your work.

Personal Life Satisfaction

It is important that therapists working with survivors of childhood trauma have nonwork outlets for developing their self-esteem and self-worth. Without these, they may bring these personal needs into their work, which is countertherapeutic for their clients.

Keeping a balance between personal and work-related interests supports therapists in their work and keeps them energized and vital. Therapists who have poor self-care skills may bring less energy to the therapy, which can become a clinical issue. Clients are very quick to pick up incongruencies between a therapist's advice about self-care and his or her own behavior in this regard. Such incongruence echoes the denial and hypocracy that surrounded the client's abuse experience and must, therefore, be avoided.

Some of the specific ways that contributors reported exercising good self-care include:

- reading novels and listening to music;
- having lots of friends who are not therapists;
- attending to spiritual needs;
- scheduling regular physical exercise;
- having supportive intimate relationships, but not using these relationships to process work-related stressors;
- going into personal therapy when necessary;
- taking regular vacations;
- limiting their work week to four days a week; and
- doing volunteer work for interesting organizations.

Clearly, each therapist's recreational and creative interests will change over time. The point is that whatever your interests are, they need to be cultivated and supported.

ISSUES FOR THERAPISTS WHO ARE THEMSELVES SURVIVORS OF SEXUAL ABUSE

Therapists who are also survivors of sexual abuse bring both assets and liabilities to their work. Having personal experience of the recovery process can help the therapist to join with clients in a profound way. Clients often feel reassured that they will be understood when they share their experience with another survivor. However, there is a risk that the therapist who is a survivor will over- or underidentify with clients whose experiences echo his or her own abuse history. This may result in over- or underworking on behalf of certain clients.

The major issue for therapists who are survivors is that they not project their own issues onto their clients. Good clinical supervision is essential so that therapists can clearly assess when issues are their own and when they belong to their clients.

It is not advisable for therapists who are survivors to provide therapy to other survivors until they are sufficiently familiar with their own abuse-related psychology that they can predict the kinds of countertransference that could arise. Knowing these vulnerabilities enables the therapist to anticipate which clients they will find most difficult to work with. When it seems necessary, such clients can be referred to another therapist.

Therapists who are survivors must develop clear self-care strategies to support themselves should they find they are being triggered by their clients' abuse-related material. These strategies include thoughtful caseload management and scheduling, supervision, techniques for bracketing personal feelings and responses during sessions with clients, and a well developed and intimate peer support network.

Therapists who are also survivors will need to give some thought to the issue of self-disclosure. Clients will frequently want to know if their therapist was abused as a child. The question for therapists to ask themselves is, "What is the therapeutic gain for my client if I disclose information about myself?" The therapist should disclose only as much information as is helpful to the client. In general, brief honest answers will satisfy the client's need for information about you and the session can then refocus on your client's agenda.

Resources

This final chapter identifies resources that contributors have used to enhance their clinical practice with male survivors and that they recommend to their clients who are recovering from sexual abuse. It is divided into three sections: video resources, written resources, and training resources. The written resources section contains materials for both therapists and clients.

This listing of resources is by no means definitive. New resources are constantly being created. In addition, many resources that were created with female sexual abuse survivors in mind can be effective tools for male survivors.

In order to keep the lists succinct, only those written resources that were recommended by two or more contributors have been included.

VIDEO RESOURCES

(Order of information: title and description followed by distributor)

Abuse

Nineteen-year-old Jeff describes the pattern of his sexual abuse, which began before he was five. After seeking professional help, he is now able to enjoy life and is restoring his self-esteem. Jeff's story shows how enduring abuse can severely damage self-esteem and impair the ability to relate to others in healthy ways. This program defines four kinds of abuse: physical, emotional, sexual, and neglect. *(20 minutes)*

> **Kidsrights**
> **10100 Park Cedar Drive**
> **Charlotte, North Carolina 28210**
> **Tel: 704-541-0100 or**
> **1-800-892-KIDS**

Big Boys Don't Cry

This excellent made-for-TV documentary explores the lives of several members of an adult male survivors group and the impact of childhood sexual victimization on them. Members share information about changes they have made in their lives since beginning therapy. Scenes from an adolescent victim/perpetrator group are interspersed with adult footage to reinforce the importance of early intervention. *(60 minutes)*

> **Public Affairs**
> **KGW TV**
> **1501 South West Jefferson Street**
> **Portland, Oregon 97201**
> **Tel: 503-226-5000**

Both Sides of the Coin

A pioneering video that brings together an adult victim of child sexual abuse and a convicted pedophile. The result is an insightful, well-rounded, and balanced examination of the causes and effects of child abuse. Two men explore the impact of child abuse on their respective lives. *(47 minutes)*

> **Kinetic Inc.**
> **408 Dundas Street East**
> **Toronto, Ontario M5A 2A5 Canada**
> **Tel: 416-963-0653**

"Breaking Silence"

This moving and personal documentary focuses on adults who were abused as children and are struggling to come to terms with their long-secret pasts. Although only adults are interviewed, their stories are interwoven with photographs of their childhood. The film deals with realities of the sexual abuse of children such as the frequency of transgenerational transmission of abusive behavior. This documentary demonstrates the difficulties abused children face as adults in integrating their painful experiences. *(58 minutes)*

> **Video and Film Rental Library**
> **American Psychiatric Association**
> **1400 K Street Northwest**
> **Washington, D.C. 20005**
> **Tel: 202-682-6173**

Coming Home: A Spiritual Recovery from Satanic Ritual Abuse

This four-part video is an edited version of a workshop on spiritual recovery that was sponsored by the Grace Institute. The subject of satanic ritual abuse is examined from both personal and theological points of view. A survivor of satanic abuse discusses her experience of rediscovering the sacred. *(120 minutes)*

> **Varied Directions International**
> **69 Elm Street**
> **Camden, Maine 04843**
> **Tel: 207-236-8506 or**
> **1-800-888-5236**

Dr. Frank Ochberg on Victimization and PTSD

This tape features an overview of Post Traumatic Stress Disorder (PTSD) by Dr. Frank Ochberg, psychiatrist and internationally noted expert on victimization and PTSD. It is an excellent program for people suffering from PTSD, their co-workers, and family members. *(15 minutes)*

> **Varied Directions International**
> **69 Elm Street**
> **Camden, Maine 04843**
> **Tel: 207-236-8506 or**
> **1-800-888-5236**

Four Men Speak Out on Surviving Child Sexual Abuse

Four male survivors, some survivors of violent, isolated assaults, others of lengthy molestations, discuss their abuse and recovery processes. The perpetrators include a father, known trusted adults, and other adolescents. The men talk about homophobia, the fear of becoming a perpetrator, and relationship issues in their adult years. Recognizing that recovery brings confusion, pain, and relief, these four men share what has been meaningful in their own healing process. *(28 minutes)*

> **Varied Directions International**
> **69 Elm Street**
> **Camden, Maine 04843**
> **Tel: 207-236-8506 or**
> **1-800-888-5236**

Healing Sexual Abuse: The Recovery Process

Dan Sexton, director of Child Help, U.S.A., and Ellen Bass (Bass & Davis, 1988), co-author of *The Courage to Heal*, discuss topics such as dissociation, addictions, regaining trust, confronting the offender, and grief. This video is recommended for both male and female survivors. *(60 minutes)*

> **Varied Directions International**
> **69 Elm Street**
> **Camden, Maine 04843**
> **Tel: 207-236-8506 or**
> **1-800-888-5236**

Partners In Healing

This video explores the dynamics of couples in various stages of therapy working together to heal the emotional scars of incest. It can help incest survivors and therapists learn how incest affects sexuality, how both partners are affected by the intimacy problems that result from incest, and how both can work together to become partners in healing. *(43 minutes)*

Varied Directions International
69 Elm Street
Camden, Maine 04843
Tel: 207-236-8506 or
1-800-888-5236

WRITTEN RESOURCES

(In addition to the books listed below, see References to locate written resources on male sexual abuse.)

For Both Therapists and Clients

Abused Boys—The Neglected Victims of Sexual Abuse. Mic Hunter *(Fawcett Columbine, 1990).*

This book is divided into two sections. The first addresses the theoretical aspects of sexual abuse and recovery and the second lets 13 male survivors speak for themselves about these issues. It is written for both clients and therapists.

For Therapists

Grown-Up Abused Children. *James Leehan and Laura Pistone Wilson (Charles C. Thomas Publishers, 1985).*

A readable and concise presentation of issues and clinical experience in group work with adult abuse survivors of both genders. It includes descriptions of typical inter- and intrapsychic dynamics of grown-up abused children, how these dynamics emerge and are expressed in therapy groups, and group interventions to help clients change.

Healing the Incest Wound: Adult Survivors in Therapy. Christine
Courtois (W.W. Norton and Company, 1988).

Provides an eloquent and thorough examination of intrafamilial
abuse dynamics and incest therapy. The book focuses on female
survivors; however, much of the theoretical information it contains
is equally applicable to both males and females.

Resolving Sexual Abuse. Yvonne Dolan (W.W. Norton & Co., 1991).

This readable and informative book discusses Ericksonian and
solution-focused approaches to working with survivors. Although
case examples are generally female, methods and techniques are
gender-neutral.

The Sexually Abused Male, Volumes 1 and 2. Mic Hunter (ed.)
(Lexington Books, 1990).

This two-volume work comprehensively examines male sexual
abuse from many points of view. Both theoretical and applied information on sexual abuse dynamics and treatment is presented. One
of its great strengths is that the chapters are written by a variety of
authors, so that an eclectic array of information and therapeutic
styles is presented.

Therapy for Adults Molested as Children: Beyond Survival. John
Briere (Springer Publishing Company, 1989).

A very useful resource for therapists working with male and
female abuse survivors. It presents a thoughtful analysis of the
impacts of childhood sexual abuse and detailed discussions of treatment models and methods. It includes informative sections on cli-
ent/therapist gender issues and therapist self-care.

For Clients

Adults Molested as Children: A Survivor's Manual for Men and Women. *Euan Bear with Peter Dimock (Safer Society Press, 1988)*.

A simple and clearly written manual for adult survivors that helps them to connect here-and-now behaviors with there-and-then events. It contains excellent advice about how to choose a therapist.

Allies in Healing. *Laura Davis (HarperCollins, 1991)*.

An excellent and essential guide for partners of sexually abused adults that also contains a great deal of useful information for survivors.

Broken Boys/Mending Men. *Stephen Gruhman-Black (Ballantine Books, 1990)*.

This personal and informative book speaks to the issues that survivors must face as they change from broken boys into mending men. The author's style is open, colloquial, and easy to read.

The Courage to Heal: A Guide for Women Survivors of Child Sexual Abuse. *Ellen Bass and Laura Davis (Harper & Row, 1988)*.

Although intended for women survivors, this book has become a bible for both male and female survivors and their therapists. It is a comprehensive and empowering resource that clearly describes how childhood defenses can become dysfunctional in adulthood. The tone of the book is friendly and open.

The Courage to Heal Workbook: For Women and Men Survivors of Child Sexual Abuse. *Laura Davis (Harper & Row, 1990)*.

An excellent self-help workbook that can be used alone or in conjunction with therapy. It presents exercises to lead survivors along the road to self-awareness and recovery. Survivors often enjoy the workbook format of this text and its structured presentation.

Don't Call It Love: Recovery from Sexual Addiction. *Patrick Carnes (Bantam Books, 1991).*

This book describes both the activities and the recovery processes of sexual addictions. It includes exercises that clients can use to increase their self-awareness and to enhance positive changes.

Male Sexuality. *Bernie Zilbergeld and John Ullman (Little, Brown, 1978).*

Examines some myths about male sexuality and presents alternative information to assist men to develop their own authentic sexual identity. The book's contents extend beyond sexuality into relationship dynamics and the role of sexuality in creating intimacy. A drawback of this book is that it discusses only heterosexual sex.

Once Upon a Time...Therapeutic Stories. *Nancy Davis (Psychological Associates of Oxon Hill, 1990).*

Inspired by Ericksonian therapeutic methods, this book contains stories aimed at restoring a client's sense of power, health, wholeness, and joy. They are tailored to specific populations (e.g., victims who become abusers, or children who were ritually abused). The stories are written for adolescents or children, but with some adaptations they can be used with adults.

Outgrowing the Pain: A Book for and about Adults Abused as Children. *Eliana Gil (Dell Publishing, 1983).*

This is a small book which describes abuse and its impacts in concise and readable terms. It also briefly describes actions survivors can take to help heal themselves. This is an excellent resource for clients in the beginning phases of therapy.

Victims No Longer: Men Recovering from Incest and Other Sexual Child Abuse. Mike Lew (Nevraumont Publishing Company, 1988). (Reprinted by Harper & Row, New York, 1990.)

A friendly and informative book that focuses specifically on male survivors. The after-effects of childhood sexual abuse and the recovery process are discussed, alongside survivors' own stories. This book can become a "good friend" to male survivors throughout their healing process.

TRAINING RESOURCES

Training resources for therapists who work with male survivors are still scarce. However, two international conferences that focus exclusively on male sexual abuse are held each year in the United States. For information on the four-day *National Male Survivors Conference*, held since 1989, contact:

Shunomi Creek Consultants
2801 Buford Highway
Suite 400
Atlanta, Georgia 30329
Tel: 404-321-4954

For information on the three-day conference *It Happens to Boys Too...*, contact:

Mr. Daniel P. Moriarty
Administrator For Personnel and
Training
St. Aloysius Home
40 Austin Avenue
Greenville, Rhode Island 02828
Tel: 401-949-1300

Appendix A

Questionnaire

The contributors to this research were asked to participate in a two-step data-collection process: the first step was to answer the questionnaire shown in this appendix; and the second step entailed participating in a semi-structured telephone interview. The questionnaire gathered preliminary information about the therapists' theoretical orientation, their experience, their clients' demographic profile, common therapeutic issues being presented by their clients, and frequently used resources.

Please answer the following questions by placing a checkmark (✓) beside the appropriate answer or by writing your answer in the space provided. Use the margins or the back of the paper if you require additional space.

Any reference to clients in the questionnaire refers to male survivors of sexual abuse.

SECTION I: THERAPIST INFORMATION

1. Name:
2. Occupation/Position:
3. Employer (if applicable):
4. Address: Phone(s):
5a. Number of years' experience of working directly with sexual abuse clients (female or male):
    ___ 0–2 years
    ___ 3–5 years

___ 6–8 years
___ more than 8 years

5b. Number of years' experience of working with male survivors of sexual abuse:
___ 0–2 years
___ 3–5 years
___ 6–8 years
___ more than 8 years

6a. Modalities in which treatment is provided to male survivors of sexual abuse:
___ individual therapy
___ group therapy
___ couple therapy
___ family therapy
___ other (please specify)

6b. Ideally, how do you sequence the above-noted treatment modalities (see question 6a) in providing treatment to male survivors of sexual abuse? In practice, do you often alter this sequence? Please discuss this below:

_____

_____

_____

_____

_____

_____

_____

_____

_____

_____

_____

_____

_____

_____

7. Briefly describe the model(s) and/or theory(s) which best describe your therapeutic approach with male survivors of sexual abuse:

_____

_____

_____

_____

_____

_____

_____

_____

_____

_____

_____

_____

8. Briefly discuss the impact of the relative genders of the therapist and client in working with male survivors of sexual abuse, as noted in your clinical experience:

_____

_____

_____

_____

_____

_____

_____

_____

_____

_____

9. Which types of education/training have you used to
    support your therapeutic work with male survivors of
    sexual abuse?
    ___ self-learning (i.e., reading journals, books, etc.)
    ___ workshops & training sessions given by other
         professionals
    ___ professional conferences
    ___ formal classroom education
    ___ other (please specify)

    _____

    _____

    _____

    _____

    _____

    _____

    _____

    _____

    _____

10. Please list any resources (written resources, videos,
    films, audio cassettes, training programs, workshop
    presenters, conferences, peer consultation groups, etc.)
    that have been particularly useful to you in supporting
    your work with male survivors of sexual abuse:

    _____

    _____

    _____

    _____

    _____

    _____

    _____

    _____

11. Please indicate how you evaluate/assess the effectiveness of your therapeutic work with your clients:
    ___ formal evaluation methods (please specify)
    ___ informal evaluation methods (please specify)

_____

_____

_____

_____

_____

_____

_____

_____

_____

_____

_____

_____

_____

_____

SECTION II: CLIENT INFORMATION

12. Please indicate the age groupings of male survivors of sexual abuse that you work with:
    ___ preschool (0–5 years)
    ___ latency age (6–12 years)
    ___ adolescent (13–19 years)
    ___ early adult (20–25 years)
    ___ adult (25 and over)

13. Please describe the treatment issues that you most commonly identify in male survivors of sexual abuse (e.g., impaired relationships, lack of trust in others, substance addictions, sexual identity issues) during the course of therapy:

_____

_____

_____

_____

_____

_____

_____

_____

_____

_____

_____

_____

_____

14. Please list resources (written resources, videos, films
    music, audio cassettes, etc.) that you use in your clinical
    work with clients, or recommend to them to use on their
    own:

_____

_____

_____

_____

_____

_____

_____

_____

_____

_____

_____

_____

SECTION III: OTHER INFORMATION

15. Please use the space below to make any further comments on your work with male survivors of sexual abuse that the previous questions have not addressed:

_____

_____

_____

_____

_____

_____

_____

_____

_____

_____

_____

_____

_____

Appendix B

Contributors

I am very pleased to be able to publicly acknowledge the assistance of the 41 therapists who were interviewed during the course of writing this book by printing their names below. Their collective knowledge and experience were fundamental to the creation of this text. Their ideas, suggestions, and questions helped to create the structure and content of Opening the Door. *Thank you, contributors!*

Mr. Paul Antrobus, Luther College, University of Regina, Regina, Saskatchewan, Canada.
Dr. Dick Berry, Thistletown Regional Centre, Rexdale, Ontario, Canada.
Dr. George Bilotta, San Francisco, California.
Ms. Debbie Bruckner, Alberta Vocational College, Calgary, Alberta, Canada.
Mr. Leonard Burnstein, Royal Ottawa Hospital, Ottawa, Ontario, Canada.
Mr. Ray Chapman, Coquitlam, British Columbia, Canada.
Mr. Lou Coppola, Family Counselling Service of Peterborough, Peterborough, Ontario, Canada.
Mr. Harry Dudley, Calgary Family Service Bureau, Calgary, Alberta, Canada.
Mr. Grant Fair, Willowdale, Ontario, Canada.
Mr. Paul Gerber, Hennepin County Home School, Minnetonka, Minnesota.
Mr. Peter Goodman, Eastwind Associates, Halifax, Nova Scotia, Canada.
Mr. Charlie Greenman, Rape and Sexual Assault Center, Minneapolis, Minnesota.

Ms. Anne Gresham, Family Life Mental Health Center, Anoka, Minnesota.

Mr. Stephen D. Grubman-Black, Wickford, Rhode Island.

Ms. Judith Halpern, Falls Church, Virginia.

Mr. Doug Harder, Cardwell Human Resources, Saskatoon, Saskatchewan, Canada.

Mr. Arthur Harold, Family Counselling Services of Peterborough, Peterborough, Ontario, Canada.

Mr. Rob Hawkings, Hamilton, Ontario, Canada.

Ms. Bobbi Hoover, Santa Clara, California.

Mr. Mic Hunter, St. Paul, Minnesota.

Mr. Michael Irving, Toronto, Ontario, Canada.

Dr. David Jackson, Department of Psychiatry, Saskatoon City Hospital, Saskatoon, Saskatchewan, Canada.

Mr. Peter E. Johnson, Alberta Vocational College, Calgary, Alberta, Canada.

Mr. Merlin Kobsa, Halton Sexual Abuse Program, Oakville, Ontario, Canada.

Mr. Len Kushnier, Family and Children's Services, London, Ontario, Canada.

Ms. Joan Lee, Executive Director, Family Counselling Service of Peterborough, Peterborough, Ontario, Canada.

Mr. Mike Lew, The Next Step Counselling, Newton Centre, Massachusetts.

Mr. Donald L. Mann, Clinical Social Worker, Portland, Oregon.

Mr. Michael McGrenra, San Francisco, California.

Mr. Paul McIntosh, London, Ontario, Canada.

Ms. Mary Meining, Seattle, Washington.

Ms. Karen Nielson, Family Service Association of Edmonton, Edmonton, Alberta, Canada

Ms. Kay Rice, St. Paul, Minnesota.

Ms. Deb Ruppert, Community Justice Initiatives, Kitchener, Ontario, Canada.

Mr. Jack Rusinoff, PHASE, St. Paul, Minnesota.

Mr. John Stasio, Boston, Massachusetts.

Mr. Paul Sterlocci, City Line Association Psychotherapists, St. Paul, Minnesota.

Dr. Robert Timms, Atlanta Center for Integrative Therapy, Atlanta, Georgia.

Mr. Timothy Wall, Counselling Co-ordinator, Klinic Community Health Centre, Winnipeg, Manitoba, Canada.

Mr. Steve Wardikowski, Family Service Bureau of Regina, Regina, Saskatchewan, Canada.

Mr. Don Wright, Vancouver Society for Male Survivors of Sexual Abuse, Vancouver, British Columbia, Canada.

Appendix C

DES*

The Dissociative Experience Scale (DES) was developed to be used with adults (persons 18 or older) to measure the frequency of dissociative experiences in their daily lives. The scale is a self-report measure. The length of the original scoring line for each question is 100 mm. Thus scores on each item could range from 1 to 100. A total score for the entire scale is determined by calculating the average score for all items (add all scores and divide by 28). A very high proportion of those respondents who score 30 or over will probably have a disorder that has a considerable dissociative component.

Readers are asked to use caution if they intend to use this scale with their clients. The DES was not constructed to be a diagnostic instrument. If a respondent has an average score of 30 or more, it indicates that conducting a full diagnostic interview would be appropriate to ascertain the type and degree of the client's dissociative experiences. Readers who are intending to use this scale, or wish to know more about it, are directed to Eve Carlson and Frank Putnam's paper "Manual for the Dissociative Experiences Scale," which fully explains the scale, its validity and reliability, its limitations, and its applications. This paper can be obtained by writing to Eve B. Carlson, Ph.D., Department of Psychology, Beloit College, 700 College Street, Beloit, WI 53511.

DIRECTIONS

This questionnaire consists of twenty-eight questions about experiences that you may have in your daily life. We are interested in how often you have these experiences. It is important, however, that your answers show how often these experiences happen to you when you **are not** under the influence of alcohol or drugs. To answer the questions, please determine to what degree the experience described in the question applies to you and circle the number to show what percentage of the time you have the experience.

Example:

0% 10% 20% 30% 40% 50% 60% 70% 80% 90% 100%
(never)   (always)

Date:_____ Age:_____ Sex: M F

1. Some people have the experience of driving a car and suddenly realizing that they don't remember what has happened during all or part of the trip. Circle a number to show what percentage of the time this happens to you.

    0% 10% 20% 30% 40% 50% 60% 70% 80% 90% 100%

2. Some people find that sometimes they are listening to someone talk and they suddenly realize that they did not hear all or part of what was said. Circle a number to show what percentage of the time this happens to you.

    0% 10% 20% 30% 40% 50% 60% 70% 80% 90% 100%

3. Some people have the experience of finding themselves in a place and have no idea how they got there. Circle a number to show what percentage of the time this happens to you.

    0% 10% 20% 30% 40% 50% 60% 70% 80% 90% 100%

4. Some people have the experience of finding themselves dressed in clothes that they don't remember putting on.

Circle a number to show what percentage of the time this happens to you.

0% 10% 20% 30% 40% 50% 60% 70% 80% 90% 100%

5. Some people have the experience of finding new things among their belongings that they do not remember buying. Circle a number to show what percentage of the time this happens to you.

0% 10% 20% 30% 40% 50% 60% 70% 80% 90% 100%

6. Some people sometimes find that they are approached by people that they do not know who call them by another name or insist that they have met before. Circle a number to show what percentage of the time this happens to you.

0% 10% 20% 30% 40% 50% 60% 70% 80% 90% 100%

7. Some people sometimes have the experience of feeling as though they are standing next to themselves or watching themselves do something and they actually see them- selves as if they were looking at another person. Circle a number to show what percentage of the time this happens to you.

0% 10% 20% 30% 40% 50% 60% 70% 80% 90% 100%

8. Some people are told that they sometimes do not recog- nize friends or family members. Circle a number to show what percentage of the time this happens to you.

0% 10% 20% 30% 40% 50% 60% 70% 80% 90% 100%

9. Some people find that they have no memory for some important events in their lives (for example, a wedding or graduation). Circle a number to show what percent- age of the time this happens to you.

0% 10% 20% 30% 40% 50% 60% 70% 80% 90% 100%

10. Some people have the experience of being accused of lying when they do not think that they have lied. Circle a number to show what percentage of the time this happens to you.

0% 10% 20% 30% 40% 50% 60% 70% 80% 90% 100%

11. Some people have the experience of looking in a mirror and not recognizing themselves. Circle a number to show what percentage of the time this happens to you.

\0% 10% 20% 30% 40% 50% 60% 70% 80% 90% 100%

12. Some people have the experince of feeling that other people, objects, and the world around them are not real. Circle a number to show what percentage of the time this happens to you.

0% 10% 20% 30% 40% 50% 60% 70% 80% 90% 100%

13. Some people have the experience of feeling that their body does not seem to belong to them. Circle a number to show what percentage of the time this happens to you.

0% 10% 20% 30% 40% 50% 60% 70% 80% 90% 100%

14. Some people have the experience of sometimes remembering a past event so vividly that they feel as if they were reliving that event. Circle a number to show what percentage of the time this happens to you.

0% 10% 20% 30% 40% 50% 60% 70% 80% 90% 100%

15. Some people have the experience of not being sure whether things that they remember happening really did happen or whether they just dreamed them. Circle a number to show what percentage of the time this happens to you.

0% 10% 20% 30% 40% 50% 60% 70% 80% 90% 100%

16. Some people have the expereince of being in a familiar place but finding it strange and unfamiliar. Circle a number to show what percentage of the time this happens to you.

0% 10% 20% 30% 40% 50% 60% 70% 80% 90% 100%

17. Some people find that when they are watching television or a movie they become so absorbed in the story that they are unaware of events happening around them. Circle a number to show what percentage of the time this happens to you.

0% 10% 20% 30% 40% 50% 60% 70% 80% 90% 100%

18. Some people find that they become so involved in a fantasy or daydream that it feels as though it werc really happening to them. Circle a number to show what percentage of the time this happens to you.

0% 10% 20% 30% 40% 50% 60% 70% 80% 90% 100%

19. Some people find that they sometimes are able to ignore pain. Circle a number to show what percentage of the time this happens to you.

0% 10% 20% 30% 40% 50% 60% 70% 80% 90% 100%

20. Some people find that they sometimes sit staring off into space, thinking of nothing, and are not aware of the passage of time. Circle a number to show what percentage of the time this happens to you.

0% 10% 20% 30% 40% 50% 60% 70% 80% 90% 100%

21. Some people find that when they are alone they talk out loud to themselves. Circle a number to show hat percentage of the time this happens to you.

0% 10% 20% 30% 40% 50% 60% 70% 80% 90% 100%

22. Some people find that in one situation they may act so differently compared with another situation that they feel almost as if they were two different people. Circle a number to show what percentage of the time this happens to you.

0% 10% 20% 30% 40% 50% 60% 70% 80% 90% 100%

23. Some people find that sometimes in certain situations they are able to do things with amazing ease and spontaneity that would usually be difficult for them (for example, sports, work, social situations, etc.). Circle a number to show what percentage of the time this happens to you.

0% 10% 20% 30% 40% 50% 60% 70% 80% 90% 100%

24. Some people sometimes find that they cannot remember whether they have done something or have just thought about doing that thing. (for example, not knowing whether they have just mailed a letter or have just thought about mailing it). Circle a number to show what percentage of the time this happens to you.

0% 10% 20% 30% 40% 50% 60% 70% 80% 90% 100%

25. Some people find evidence that they have done things that they do not remember doing. Circle a number to show what percentage of the time this happens to you.

0% 10% 20% 30% 40% 50% 60% 70% 80% 90% 100%

26. Some people sometimes find writings, drawings, or notes among their belongings that they must have done but cannot remember doing. Circle a number to show what percentage of the time this happens to you.

0% 10% 20% 30% 40% 50% 60% 70% 80% 90% 100%

27. Some people sometimes find that they hear voices inside their head that tell them to do things or comment on things that they are doing. Circle a number to show what percentage of the time this happens to you.

    0% 10% 20% 30% 40% 50% 60% 70% 80% 90% 100%

28. Some people sometimes feel as if they are looking at the world through a fog so that people and objects appear far away or unclear. Circle a number to show what percentage of the time this happens to you.

    0% 10% 20% 30% 40% 50% 60% 70% 80% 90% 100%

Appendix D

Intervention to Manage Flashbacks and Intervention to Ground Clients in Here-and-Now Experience

The following two interventions were developed by Yvonne Dolan and are reprinted with the permission of the author and her publisher. Readers who find these interventions useful and wish to learn others like them are directed to Ms. Dolan's excellent book, Resolving Sexual Abuse *(New York: W.W. Norton), copyright* © *by Yvonne M. Dolan.*

INTERVENTION TO MANAGE FLASHBACKS (FOUR-STEP APPROACH TO DEALING WITH FLASHBACKS IN DAILY LIFE)

The following four steps will help the client experience more understanding and resulting control of her flashback experiences both in and outside the therapy setting:

1. "Describe what you are experiencing. When have you felt this way before? What situation were you in the last time you felt this way?"*

2. "In what ways are this current situation and your past situation similar? For example, is the setting, time of year, or the sights, sounds, sensations in any way similar to the past situation where you felt this way? If there is another person involved, is she or he similar to a person from the past who elicited similar feelings?"

3. "How is your current situation different from the situation in which you felt similar feelings in the past? What is different about you, your sensory experience, your current life circumstances, and personal resources? What is different about this current setting? If another person or persons are involved, what is different about them compared to the person(s) in the past situation?"

4. "What action, if any, do you want to take now to feel better in the present?" (For example, a flashback may indicate that a person is once again in a situation that is in some way unsafe. If this is the case, self-protective actions should be taken to alter the current situation. On the other hand, a flashback may simply mean that an old memory has been triggered by an inconsequential but highly evocative resemblance to the past such as a certain color, smell, sound, etc. In such cases, corrective messages of reassurance and comfort need to be given to the self to counteract old traumatic memories. Associational cues for comfort and security are useful for this purpose.)

INTERVENTION TO GROUND CLIENTS IN HERE-AND-NOW EXPERIENCE

This intervention uses clients' hypervigilance to assist them to relax and become centered in their present environment.

---

*If the client is unable to identify when she has felt this way before, unconscious resources can be elicited to help her gain the necessary information and understanding for resolution.

Clients who are dissociated, or who wish to induce physical relaxation, are instructed to:

- Name 5 things that you see
- Name 5 things that you hear
- Name 5 things that you feel
- Name 4 things that you see
- Name 4 things that you hear
- Name 4 things that you feel
- Name 3 things that you see
  Etc.
- Name 2 things that you see
  Etc.
- Name 1 thing that you see
  Etc.

Each time the client identifies something that he sees, hears, or feels, he should say "I see..., I see..., I see..., I sec..., I see..., I hear..., I hear..., I hear..., etc." This rhythmic repetition is relaxing and calming.

The same object, sound, or feeling can be named twice, or more, in a row. This is quite acceptable. The exercise can be done in silence or out loud. It can be repeated as often as necessary. The client can lose his place in the exercise; he just begins again where he thinks that he left off.

This technique works best if the client is sitting down or stationary. It can be conducted in busy or quiet surroundings. It should not be conducted while one is driving a vehicle.

Appendix E

Behaviors That Support Group Process

This handout was developed by the Halton Sexual Abuse Treatment Program in Oakville, Ontario, Canada, and it is reprinted with their kind permission.

GOOD GROUP EXPERIENCES DON'T JUST HAPPEN! They are the result of the commitment and involvement of the participants. We will be spending a number of hours together. You will be free to talk about yourself as much or as little as you wish. No effort will be made to force anyone to tell more about himself that he wishes to. Would you, therefore, read, think about, and discuss the qualities of good group interchange listed below?

1. **SHARING IS ESSENTIAL**. Your thoughts, feelings, and experiences are the life-stuff of this group. We all need them in order that insights may be discovered, understanding deepened, and growth achieved.
2. **Express FEELINGS, not just ideas.** Feelings are the best indicators of what people value. To do this, you must be in touch with your feelings. Take time to reflect on them and try to identify them clearly.
3. **Expressing NEGATIVE FEELINGS can, on occasion, also be helpful**. Unexpressed feelings simply set up blocks or dribble away in unproductive ways.
4. **Respect, care about, and SUPPORT EACH PERSON**

IN THE GROUP. The more confidence each feels, the more anxiety diminishes and the more deeply we can explore the topics before us.

5. **SUPPORT NEEDS TO BE EXPRESSED.** Don't presume that people somehow know you are feeling supportive. They won't, unless you show that you are.

6. **PUTTING PEOPLE DOWN CLOSES PEOPLE UP and is counterproductive.**

7. **POSITIVE CONFRONTATION IS ACCEPTABLE and needed.** To confront means to present someone with a new or opposing idea for the sake of acknowledgement, agreement, contradiction, or clarification. It identifies where people stand and shows what they consider important.

8. **Confront others with their unused STRENGTHS as well as their weaknesses.** Confront in order to help another grow.

9. **Accusation and ridicule will only engender HOSTILITY and set up blocks.** Avoid them.

10. **AVOID FORCING YOUR VIEWPOINT BY AN OVERBEARING ATTITUDE or barrage of arguments.**

11. **OUR GROUP GOAL IS NOT WINNING, BUT GROWING.** Don't water down your positions, but do state them in a way that allows people room for maneuver and positive response.

12. **Try to AVOID BECOMING DEFENSIVE.** Realize you are among friends. View confrontations as an invitation to self-exploration.

13. **Fruitful discussion requires OPENNESS TO CHANGE.**

14. **STICK TO THE POINT.** Don't wander.

15. **SPEAK FOR YOURSELF.** Avoid using "We" when you mean "I." Don't speak for the group without giving others a chance to agree or disagree.

16. **DON'T USE "I" SUBSTITUTES** such as "One would think" or "Any rational person would agree." Take responsibility for what you say.

17. **MOSTLY SPEAK ABOUT YOURSELF.** Growth occurs chiefly when the group applies the topic to their own lives.

18. **MOSTLY SPEAK TO INDIVIDUALS.** A series of monologues to the entire group can be deadly.
19. **HELP OTHERS EXPLORE AND DEVELOP** the ideas and feelings they are expressing.
20. **YOU ARE NEITHER THERAPIST NOR JUDGE.** Your role is not to set other people straight or to solve their problems, but to share, help, and encourage.
21. **EXPRESS DISAGREEMENTS AS YOUR IDEA,** not as absolute truth. Find common ground and areas of agreement before setting forth points of difference.
22. **SAY IT IN THE GROUP.** The things you say to your friends about the group before, after, or between meetings are often the very things which should be said in the group. There should be only one conversation at a time going on in the group.
23. **MAKE THE MEETINGS.** If one person misses a meeting, the dynamics of the group change; and it often happens that the one who was absent cannot be brought up to date because he did not experience what really happened. The group needs to have you present.
24. **ENJOY YOURSELVES.** Life is too short to spend time doing things you don't like. Help others enjoy themselves through warmth, friendship, and caring.

Appendix F

Dean Adolescent Inventory Scale*

Dr. Gwen Dean developed this self-report scale to help identify adolescent dissociation, and it is reprinted here with her permission. It is included in this text to help clinicians identify any dissociative behaviors their adolescent clients may be exhibiting. Readers are cautioned that although using this scale may help assess adolescent dissociation, it is not intended to replace a full diagnostic interview.

Circle One

1. I have been afraid to tell anybody about some of my experiences. TRUE FALSE

2. Sometimes I hear arguing in my head and if confuses me. TRUE FALSE

3. When I was very young, I pretended to have a playmate that nobody knew about. TRUE FALSE

4. Sometimes when I am writing I feel like someone else is guiding my hand. TRUE FALSE

5. Often times when I look into the
    mirror my haircolor seems to
    change.   TRUE   FALSE

6. When I am eating food, there
    are times that "I" cannot taste
    the food.   TRUE   FALSE

7. When I am playing sports with
    friends, sometimes I can do real
    well in one game and then the
    next time I play it I feel like the
    game is new to me.   TRUE   FALSE

8. Sometimes when I sleep at
    night I feel like I am awake
    and I am having conversations
    with people.   TRUE   FALSE

9. I am upset when people claim
    they know me and I have never
    met them before.   TRUE   FALSE

10. My handwriting changes often.   TRUE   FALSE

11. I have looked into the mirror
    and have seen someone other
    than myself.   TRUE   FALSE

12. Something terrible happened to
    me but I don't know what it
    was.   TRUE   FALSE

13. I don't remember a lot of things
    that other people tell me
    happened to me.   TRUE   FALSE

14. Sometimes I will be with friends
    and I can't remember how I got
    there.   TRUE   FALSE

15. I feel like I have totally lost a
    portion of my memory.   TRUE   FALSE

16. When I get dressed I have a
    difficult time deciding what to

wear because it seems like parts of me want to wear something different than what I want to wear.   TRUE   FALSE

17. I have heard that people who hear voices in their heads are crazy and sometimes I think I may be crazy because I have heard voices too.   TRUE   FALSE

18. I feel like nobody has ever been able to help me.   TRUE   FALSE

19. I have bad headaches and nobody has been able to find out why.   TRUE   FALSE

20. I feel that there are things that happened to me that I could never tell anyone, but I don't know what they are.   TRUE   FALSE

21. My legs and arms and sometimes my hands move and I don't move them.   TRUE   FALSE

22. I have watched myself doing things and talking to people but could not talk.   TRUE   FALSE

23. Time is discontinuous for me.   TRUE   FALSE

24. I do lots of things at once and don't really understand how I can do this.   TRUE   FALSE

25. I have been accused of stealing but I know that I have never stolen anything.   TRUE   FALSE

26. Things have appeared in my room that I am accused of stealing but I know that I did not steal them.   TRUE   FALSE

27. My parents tell me I lie all the time. TRUE FALSE

28. I like to lie. TRUE FALSE

29. I have stolen things to get my parents mad. TRUE FALSE

30. I like to cause trouble for people. TRUE FALSE

31. Sometimes I can watch myself getting into trouble and I can't stop it. TRUE FALSE

32. My vision changes all the time but nobody believes me. TRUE FALSE

33. I have eaten entire meals and don't remember eating. TRUE FALSE

34. I have favorite things in my room at home, but I feel some of the things belong to someone else. TRUE FALSE

35. My parents have accused me of talking to myself. TRUE FALSE

36. I have been abused by many people. TRUE FALSE

37. Sometimes when I go to school I am not aware of what the teacher is talking about as if I had lost part of the lecture. TRUE FALSE

38. In school I have a bad memory for subjects that I thought I knew well. TRUE FALSE

39. There is a violent part of me that I have not told my doctor about. TRUE FALSE

40. Sometimes I feel like I may have done something terrible

but I don't know what it could be. TRUE FALSE

41. I panic when I get around certain people and I don't know why. TRUE FALSE

42. I have had several times when I was not sure who I was or even what my name was. TRUE FALSE

43. Sometimes I call myself by another name. TRUE FALSE

44. I always pretend that I remember things even though I just can't remember them. TRUE FALSE

45. Sometimes I am talking to a friend and I don't know what happens but I just disappear and come out later somewhere else. TRUE FALSE

46. People tell me I stare a lot. TRUE FALSE

47. My teachers in school are always trying to get my attention. TRUE FALSE

48. Many times I feel that when people are talking to me they are talking to someone else. TRUE FALSE

49. Oncc I saw a person killed in real life. TRUE FALSE

50. I hide things from myself all the time. TRUE FALSE

51. My friends don't really care about me because they don't really know who I am. TRUE FALSE

52. I have witnessed someone dying in real life. TRUE FALSE

53. I don't like to talk about
    anything that causes me to get
    upset because sometimes it
    makes me disappear into myself.   TRUE   FALSE

54. When I disappear into myself I
    can hear people calling me but I
    have no control to speak out,
    and this scares me a lot.   TRUE   FALSE

55. I have been raped and can't talk
    about it.   TRUE   FALSE

56. My biggest fear is that someone
    will hurt me.   TRUE   FALSE

57. Sometimes I am working on an
    activity and then I just can't think
    at all about what I was doing
    because my mind is blank.   TRUE   FALSE

58. I have become full of rage and
    have not been able to
    understand why.   TRUE   FALSE

59. I have been told that I roll my
    eyes.   TRUE   FALSE

60. Sometimes I want to do one
    thing and my body seems to
    want to do another thing.   TRUE   FALSE

61. If I can ever find out what is
    wrong with me I will work
    hard to get better.   TRUE   FALSE

62. Some people think I am a
    problem to society but they
    can't help me either.   TRUE   FALSE

63. Sometimes I find myself
    eating food that I don't like.   TRUE   FALSE

64. I can't always smell odors even
    when I don't have a cold.   TRUE   FALSE

65. Sometimes I answer questions on exams and don't know where the answer comes from.   TRUE   FALSE

66. I have been involved in cult activities and it scares me to admit it.   TRUE   FALSE

67. I have been threatened to keep a big secret.   TRUE   FALSE

68. I have lost days at a time and have no explanation for it.   TRUE   FALSE

69. Most people that have tried to help me don't ask me the right questions about myself.   TRUE   FALSE

70. I have been constantly present during the taking of this test.   TRUE   FALSE

71. There is a part of me that is childlike and I am embarrassed when people tell me I acted that way again.   TRUE   FALSE

72. I have been told by someone in me to do things that I am not willing to do.   TRUE   FALSE

73. I rarely see things that aren't there.   TRUE   FALSE

74. Voices in my head sometimes are so clear I am frightened by them.   TRUE   FALSE

75. I feel good about taking this test because I feel like you may be able to help me.   TRUE   FALSE

76. Sometimes I feel like there are many different parts to me.   TRUE   FALSE

77. I get upset when I am extremely angry with someone I love and

I can't explain what happened
because I don't know. TRUE FALSE

78. I have tried to use drugs to
cover up my experiences. TRUE FALSE

79. There is one part of me who
wants to use drugs and I try to
keep that part under control. TRUE FALSE

80. I have heard voices in my head
that have convinced me to kill
myself. TRUE FALSE

81. Sometimes I burst out laughing
and can't stop. TRUE FALSE

82. I find myself crying and don't
understand why my eyes are
wet because "I" wasn't crying. TRUE FALSE

83. Many times I have no feeling in
part of my body and I can't
explain why. TRUE FALSE

84. I have found letters that I don't
remember writing but they were
signed by me. TRUE FALSE

85. The question that upset me the
most was question No. _____. TRUE FALSE

86. I don't remember taking this
test before. TRUE FALSE

87. My biggest fear today is that
nobody will find out what is
wrong with me then I will
think I really am crazy. TRUE FALSE

88. I believe that when I was a
small child something happened
to me that may have caused me
to do these strange things. TRUE FALSE

89. I have to be reminded many times about things that I should have done that I thought I did.   TRUE   FALSE

90. There are some people that I need to stay away from because I have thought about killing them.   TRUE   FALSE

91. I have been beaten severely.   TRUE   FALSE

92. Part of my body works at times and I can't get the other part to move.   TRUE   FALSE

93. I cover up a lot for myself because I don't know the truth anymore.   TRUE   FALSE

94. I don't think anybody has my experiences and knowing that frightens me.   TRUE   FALSE

95. I know that I do not lie to my parents, but they tell me I lie all the time.   TRUE   FALSE

96. Sometimes I feel like I am asleep all day and another part of me took over and participated in the day for me.   TRUE   FALSE

97. I will be very happy if you find out what is wrong with me.   TRUE   FALSE

98. I don't want any of my friends to know about my problem.   TRUE   FALSE

99. I have never really felt a feeling, I just pretend I do.   TRUE   FALSE

100. I feel I have lost control over myself and I need help.   TRUE   FALSE

Please write out any statements about your experience that you want your doctor to know.

_____

_____

_____

_____

_____

_____

Date of Birth: _____

Sex: M   F

Height: _____

Weight: _____

Last Grade Completed: _____

Date Test Taken: _____

References

Adams-Tucker, Christine. "Proximate Effects of Sexual Abuse in Childhood: A Report on 28 Children." *American Journal of Psychiatry*. v.139. 1982. 1252–1256.

Alexander, Pamela C. and Shirley L. Lupfer. "Family Characteristics and Long-term Consequences Associated with Sexual Abuse." *Archives of Sexual Behaviour*. v.16. 1987. 235–245.

American Humane Association. (1986). *Highlights of the official child neglect and abuse reporting, 1986*. Denver, CO: American Association for Protecting Children.

Awad, George A. "Father-Son Incest: A Case Report." *Journal of Nervous and Mental Disease*. v.162. 1976. 135–139.

Badgley, Robin, et al. *Sexual Offences in Canada: A Summary Report of the Committee on Sexual Offences Against Children and Youths*. Ottawa, Ontario: Supply and Services, 1984.

Baker, Anthony W. "Child Sexual Abuse: A Study of Prevalence in Great Britain." *Child Abuse and Neglect*. v.9. 1985. 457–467.

Banning, Anne. "Mother-Son Incest: Confronting a Prejudice." *Child Abuse and Neglect*. v.13. 1989. 563–570.

Bass, Ellyn and Laura Davis. *The Courage to Heal*. New York: Harper & Row, 1988.

Blanchard, Geral. "Male Victims of Child Sexual Abuse: A Portent of Things to Come." *Journal of Independent Social Work*. v.1. 1987. 19–27.

Briere, John. *Therapy for Adults Molested as Children: Beyond Survival*. New York: Springer Publishing Company, 1989.

Briere, John, Diane Evans, Marsha Runtz and Timothy Wall. "Symptomatology in Men Who Were Molested as Children: A Comparison Study." *American Journal of Orthopsychiatry*. v.58. 1988. 457–461.

Briere, John and Marsha Runtz. "Symptomatology Associated with Childhood Sexual Victimization in a Nonclinical Adult Sample." *Child Abuse and Neglect*. v.12. 1988. 51-59.

Brown, Jeff. "The Treatment of Male Victims with Mixed Gender, Short-Term Group Psychotherapy." ch.7 in *The Sexually Abused Male*. v.2. (Mic Hunter, ed.) Lexington, MA: Lexington Books, 1990.

Bruckner, Debra F. and Peter E. Johnson. "Treatment for Adult Male Victims of Childhood Sexual Abuse." *Social Casework*. February 1987. 81–87.

Carlson, Eve Bernstein and Frank W. Putnam. *Manual for the Dissociative Experiences Scale*. August 1992.

Carlson, Shirley "The Victim/Perpetrator: Turning Points." ch.12 in *The Sexually Abused Male*. v.2. (Mic Hunter, ed.) Lexington, MA: Lexington Books, 1990.

Condy, Sylvia Robbins, Donald I. Templer, Ric Brown and Lelia Veaco. "Parameters of Sexual Contact of Boys with Women." *Archives of Sexual Behavior*. v.16. 1987. 379–394.

Constantine, Larry L. "The Effects of Early Sexual Experiences: A Review and Synthesis of Research." ch.17 in *Children and Sex: New Findings, New Perspectives*. (L.L. Constantine and F.M. Martinson, eds.) Boston: Little, Brown & Co., 1979.

Courtois, Christine A. *Healing the Incest Wound: Adult Survivors in Therapy*. New York: W.W. Norton & Co., 1988.

Courtois, Christine A. "Theory, Sequencing and Strategy in Treating Adult Survivors." *New Directions for Mental Health Services*. Fall, 1991. 47–59.

Crowder, Adrienne and Judy Myers-Avis. *Group Treatment for Sexually Abused Adolescents*. Holmes Beach, FL: Learning Publications, 1993.

Davis, Laura. *Allies in Healing*. New York: HarperCollins, 1991.

Davis, Laura. *The Courage to Heal Workbook*. New York: Harper & Row, 1990.

Davis, Nancy. *Once Upon a Time—Therapeutic Stories*. Oxon Hill, MD: Psychological Associates of Oxon Hill, 1990.

deYoung, Mary. "Self-Injurious Behaviour in Incest Victims: A Research Note." *Child Welfare*. v.61. 1982. 577–583.

Dimock, Peter T. "Adult Males Sexually Abused as Children." *Journal of Interpersonal Violence*. v.3. 1988. 203–221.

Dixon, Katharine N., Eugene Arnold and Kenneth Calestro. "Father-Son Incest: Under-reported Psychiatric Problem?" *American Journal of Psychiatry*. v.135. July, 1978. 835–838.

Dolan, Yvonne. *Resolving Sexual Abuse*. New York: W.W. Norton & Co., 1991.

Doll, Lynda S., Dan Joy, Brad N. Bartholow, Janet S. Harrison, Gail Bolan, John M. Douglas, Linda E. Saltzman, Patricia M. Moss and Wanda Delgado. "Self-Reported Childhood and Adolescent Sexual Abuse Among Adult Homosexual and Bisexual Men." *Child Abuse and Neglect*. v.16. 1992. 855–864.

Evans, Mark C. "Brother to Brother: Integrating Concepts of Healing Regarding Male Sexual Assault Survivors and Vietnam Veterans." ch.12 in *The Sexually Abused Male*. v.2. (Mic Hunter, ed.) Lexington, MA: Lexington Books, 1990.

Everstine, Diana Sullivan and Louis Everstine. *Sexual Trauma in Children and Adolescents: Dynamics and Treatment*. New York: Brunner/Mazel Inc., 1989.

Finkelhor, David. "Boys as Victims." ch. 10 in *Child Sexual Abuse New Theory and Research*. New York: Free Press, 1984.

Finklehor, David, S. Araji, L. Baron, A. Browne, S. Peters, & G. Wyatt. *A sourcebook on child sexual abuse*. Newbury Park, CA: Sage, 1986.

Forseth, Laura B. and Art Brown. "A Survey of Interfamilial Sexual Abuse Treatment Centres: Implications for Intervention." *Child Abuse and Neglect*. v.5. 1981. 177–186.

Freeman-Longo, Robert E. "The Impact of Sexual Victimization on Males." *Child Abuse & Neglect*. v.10. 1986. 411–414.

Freund, Kurt, Robin Watson and Robert Dickey. "Does Sexual Abuse in Childhood Cause Pedophilia: An Exploratory Study." *Archives of Sexual Behaviour.* v.19. 1990. 557–568.

Friedrich, William N., Robert L. Beilke and Anthony J. Urquiza. "Behaviour Problems in Young Sexually Abused Boys." *Journal of Interpersonal Violence.* v.3. 1988. 21–28.

Fritz, Gregory S., Kim Stoll and Nathaniel N. Wagner. "A Comparison of Males and Females Who were Sexually Molested as Children." *Journal of Sex and Marital Therapy.* v.7. 1981. 54–59.

Fromuth, Mary Ellen and Barry R. Burkhart. "Long-term Psychological Correlates of Childhood Sexual Abuse in Two Samples of College Men." *Child Abuse & Neglect.* v.13. 1989. 533–542.

Froning, Mary L. and Susan B. Mayman. "Identification and Treatment of Child and Adolescent Male Victims of Sexual Abuse." ch.10 in *The Sexually Abused* Male. v.2. (Mic Hunter, ed.) Lexington, Mass: Lexington Books, 1990.

Frosh, Stephen. "No Man's Land?: The Role of Men Working with Sexually Abused Children." *British Journal of Guidance and Counselling.* v.16. 1988. 1–10.

Gerber, Paul N. "The Assessment Interview for Young Male Victims" ch. 11 in *The Sexually Abused Male.* v.1. (Mic Hunter, ed.) Lexington, MA: Lexington Books, 1990a.

Gerber, Paul N. "Victims Becoming Offenders: A Study of Ambiguities." ch.7 in *The Sexually Abused Male.* v.1. (Mic Hunter, ed.) Lexington, MA: Lexington Books, 1990b.

Gordon, Linda & Paul O'Keefe. "Incest as a Form of Family Violence: Evidence from Historical Case Records." *Journal of Marriage and the Family.* 1984. 27–34.

Gresham, Anne M. "The Role of the Nonoffending Parent When the Incest Victim is Male." ch.8 in *The Sexually Abused Male.* v.2. (Mic Hunter, ed.) Lexington, MA: Lexington Books, 1990.

Groth, Nicholas and Ann Wolbert Burgess. "Male Rape: Offenders and Victims." *American Journal of Psychiatry.* v.137. 1980. 806–810.

Grubman-Black, Stephen D. *Broken Boys/Mending Men: Recovery from Childhood Sexual Abuse.* New York: Ballantine Books, 1990.

Halpern, Judith. "Family Therapy in Father-Son Incest: A Case Study." *Social Casework.* 1987. 88–93.

Hunter, Mic. *Abused Boys—The Neglected Victims of Sexual Abuse.* New York: Fawcett Columbine, 1990a.

Hunter, Mic. (ed). *The Sexually Abused Male.* 2 vols. Lexington, MA: Lexington Books, 1990b.

Hunter, Mic and Paul N. Gerber. "Use of the Terms 'Victim' and 'Survivor' in the Grief Stages Commonly Seen During Recovery from Sexual Abuse." ch.3 in *The Sexually Abused Male.* v.2. (Mic Hunter, ed.) Lexington, MA: Lexington Books, 1990.

Janus, Mark-David, Ann W. Burgess and Arlene McCormack. "Histories of Sexual Abuse in Adolescent Male Runaways." *Adolescence.* v.22. 1987.

405–417.

Johnson, Robert L. and Diane Shrier. "Past Sexual Victimization by Females of Male Patients in an Adolescent Medicine Clinic Population." *American Journal of Psychiatry.* v.144. 1987. 650–652.

Jones, Robert J., Kenneth J. Gruber and Mary H. Freeman. "Reactions of Adolescents to Being Interviewed About Their Sexual Assault Experiences." *Journal of Sex Research.* v.19. 1983. 160–172.

Kaplan, Meg S., Judith V. Becker and Craig E. Tenke. "Influence of Abuse History on Male Adolescent Self-Reported Comfort with Interviewer Gender." *Journal of Interpersonal Violence.* v.6. 1991. 3–11.

Kaufman, Arthur, Peter Divasto, Rebecca Jackson, Dayton Voorhees and Joan Christy. "Male Rape Victims: Non-institutionalized Assault." *American Journal of Psychiatry.* v.137. 1980. 221–223.

Kilgore, Laurie C. "Effect of Early Childhood Sexual Abuse on Self and Ego Development." *Social Casework.* April, 1988. 224–230.

Langevin, Ron, P. Wright and L. Handy. "Characteristics of Sex Offenders Who Were Sexually Victimized as Children." *Annals of Sex Research.* v.2. 227–253.

Leehan, James and Laura Pistone Wilson. *Grown-up Abused Children.* Springfield, IL: Charles C. Thomas, 1985.

Lew, Mike. *Victims No Longer: Men Recovering from Incest and Other Sexual Child Abuse.* New York: Harper & Row, 1988.

Marshall, W.L., H.E. Barbaree and Jennifer Butt. "Sexual Offenders Against Male Children: Sexual Preferences." *Behavioral Research and Theory.* v.26. 1988. 383–391.

McCormack, Arlene, Mark-David Janus and Ann Wolbert Burgess. "Runaway Youths and Sexual Victimization: Gender Differences in an Adolescent Runaway Population." *Child Abuse and Neglect.* v.10. 1986. 387–395.

Metcalfe, Michael, Rhonda Oppenheimer, Andree Dignon and R.L. Palmer. "Childhood Sexual Experiences Reported by Male Psychiatric Patients." *Psychological Medicine.* v.20. 1990. 925–929.

Myers, Michael F. "Men Sexually Assaulted as Adults and Sexually Abused as Boys." *Archives of Sexual Behaviour.* v.18. no.3. 1989. 203–215.

Nielsen, Terry Ann. "Sexually Abuse of Boys: Current Perspectives." *The Personnel and Guidance Journal.* November, 1983. 139–142.

O'Connor, Art. "Female Sex Offenders." *British Journal of Psychiatry.* v.150. 1987. 615–620.

Olson, Peter E. "The Sexual Abuse of Boys: A Study of the Long-Term Psychological Effects." ch.6 in *The Sexually Abused Male.* v.1. (Mic Hunter, ed.) Lexington, MA: Lexington Books, 1990.

Paitich, D., R. Langevin, R. Freeman, K. Mann and L. Handy. "The Clarke SHQ: A Clinical Sex History Questionnaire for Males." *Archives of Sexual Behaviour.* v.6. 1977, 421–436.

Parker, Stephen. "Healing Abuse in Gay Men: The Group Component." ch. 9 in *The Sexually Abused Male.* v.2. (Mic Hunter, ed.) Lexington MA: Lexington Books, 1990.

Pierce, Lois H. "Father-Son Incest: Using the Literature to Guide Practice."

Social Casework. February, 1987. 67–74.

Pierce, Robert and Lois Hauck Pierce. "The Sexually Abused Child: A Comparison of Male and Female Victims." *Child Abuse and Neglect*. v.9. 1985. 191–199.

Reinhart, Michael A. "Sexually Abused Boys." *Child Abuse and Neglect*. v.11. 1987. 229–235.

Risin, Leslie and Mary P. Koss. "The Sexual Abuse of Boys: Prevalence and Descriptive Characteristics of Childhood Victimizations." *Journal of Interpersonal Violence*. v.2. 1987. 309–323.

Rose, Deborah S. "'Worse than Death': Psychodynamics of Rape Victims and the Need for Psychotherapy." *The American Journal of Psychiatry*. v.143. 1986. 817–824.

Sandfort, Theodorus G.M. "Sex in Pedophiliac Relationships: An Empirical Investigation Among a Non-representative Group of Boys." *Journal of Sex Research*. v.20. 1984. 123–142.

Sarrel, Philip and William H. Masters. "Sexual Molestation of Men by Women." *Archives of Sexual Behaviour*. v.11. 1982. 117–131.

Schacht, Anita J., Daniel Kerlinsky and Cindy Carlson. "Group Therapy with Sexually Abused Boys: Leadership, Projective Identification and Countertransference Issues." *International Journal of Group Psychotherapy*. v.40. 1990. 401–417.

Sebold, John. "Indicators of Child Sexual Abuse in Males." *The Journal of Contemporary Social Work*. February, 1987. 75–80.

Sepler, Fran. "Victim Advocacy and Young Male Victims of Sexual Abuse: An Evolutionary Model." ch. 3 in *The Sexually Abused Male*. v.1. (Mic Hunter, ed.) Lexington, MA: Lexington Books, 1991.

Steele, Katherine and Joanna Colrain. "Abreactive Work with Sexual Abuse Survivors: Concepts and Techniques." ch.1 in *The Sexually Abused Male*. v.2. (Mic Hunter, ed.) Lexington, MA: Lexington Books, 1990.

Struve, Jim. "Dancing with the Patriarchy: The Politics of Sexual Abuse." ch.1 in *The Sexually Abused Male*. v.1. (Mic Hunter, ed.) Lexington, MA: Lexington Books, 1990.

Summit, Roland C. "The Child Sexual Abuse Accommodation Syndrome." *Child Abuse and Neglect*. v.7. 1983. 177–193.

Swift, Carolyn. "The Prevention of Sexual Child Abuse: Focus on the Perpetrator." *Journal of Clinical Child Psychology*. Summer, 1979. 133–136.

Timms, Robert and Patrick Connors. "Integrating Psychotherapy and Body Work for Abuse Survivors: A Psychological Model." ch.6 in *The Sexually Abused Male*. v.2. (Mic Hunter, ed.) Lexington, MA: Lexington Books, 1990.

Tindall, Ralph H. "The Male Adolescent Involved with a Pederast Becomes an Adult." *Journal of Homosexuality*. v.3. 1978. 373–382.

Trivelpiece, James W. "Adjusting the Frame: Cinematic Treatment of Sexual Abuse and Rape of Men and Boys." ch.2 in *The Sexually Abused Male*. v.1. (Mic Hunter, ed.) Lexington, MA: Lexington Books. 1990.

Urquiza, Anthony J. and Lisa Marie Keating. "The Prevalence of Sexual Victimization of Males." ch.4 in *The Sexually Abused Male*. v.1. (Mic Hunter, ed.) Lexington, MA: Lexington Books, 1990.

Urquiza, Anthony J. and Maria Capra. "The Impact of Sexual Abuse: Initial and Long-Term Effects." ch.5 in *The Sexually Abused Male*. v.1. (Mic Hunter, ed.) Lexington, MA: Lexington Books, 1990.

Vander May, Brenda J. "The Sexual Victimization of Male Children: A Review of Previous Research." *Child Abuse and Neglect*. v.12. 1988. 61–72.

Zilbergeld, Bernie and John Ullman. *Male Sexuality*. Boston: Little, Brown & Co., 1978.

Index

Abreaction(s), 54, 81, 85, 86, 97, 107, 127, 143
  definition of, 92–93
Absorption, 68
Abuse. *See also* Addiction
  drawing of. *See* Drawing
  emotional, 19
  physical. *See* Physical abuse
  sexual. *See* Sexual abuse
  therapeutic process as isomorphic to, 1, 41, 58, 98
Abuser. *See* Offender(s)
Abuse-reactive life decisions, 42
Abuse-reactive perpetration, 14, 29–31, 66–67, 83–84, 105, 126
Abuse-related material, in group, 107
Abusive relationships, 61, 118
Acceptance
  grief and, 47
  by therapist, 49
Accountability
  of client, 31, 83, 130
  of offender, 79
Achievement, of goals, 67
Acting out, 38, 81, 86, 126, 130, 132
  symbolic, 82
  by therapist, 138
Active participation, in group, 109
Activities, sexual, types of, 17–18, 36, 63
Adaptive living strategies, 81. *See also* Coping strategies
Addiction, 23, 99, 105
  drug, 23, 46, 84
  food, 23, 84
  process, 23, 52, 61
  sexual, 23, 31–32, 84–85, 154
  sports, 23
  substance, 23, 52, 61
  work, 23, 84
Adolescents
  assessment of, 128–130
  counselling of, 125–135

and female therapist, 121, 131
  treatment process with, 131–135
Adult identity, symbols of, 91
Advocacy, 144
Affect. *See also* Emotions; Feelings
  blocking of, 85
  repression of, 23, 26, 46, 72, 81, 85–86, 87, 92, 97, 102
Affection, nonsexual, 102
Affective components, of abuse, 38, 53, 92
Affective expression
  in group, 109
  increasing of, 85–90, 93
Affective improvements, 67
Agencies
  child protection. *See* Child protection agencies
  treatment, 14, 31
Age regressions, 93
Aggression
  by offender, 47
  by victim, 15, 29–31, 32, 33, 38, 66, 132
Aggressors, alters as, 26
Alcohol, 23, 46, 84
Altered states of consciousness, 92
Alters, 26–27, 91, 92, 105, 106, 120
Ambivalence, toward abuser, 87
American Humane Association, 10
Amnestic dissociation, 68
Anal sex, 65
Anchors, 74, 75–76, 93
Anger, 21, 23–24, 38, 39, 63, 82, 84, 86, 87, 88, 89, 102, 119, 120, 125, 132, 134
  grief and, 47
  of therapist, 141
Anger releases, bioenergetic, 89
Antisocial behavior, 38. *See also* Delinquency; Noncompliance
Anxiety, 23, 33, 42, 51, 52, 60, 65, 66,